Writing SIMULATIONS

Challenging

Written by Mari Lu Robbins, M.A.

Teacher Created Materials, Inc.
P.O. Box 1040
Huntington Beach, CA 92647
©1997 Teacher Created Materials, Inc.
Made in U.S.A.

ISBN 1-57690-121-1

Edited by
Walter Kelly
Cover Art by
Sue Fullam
José Tapia

Teacher Created Materials

Table of Contents

Introduction

The ability to write well is a skill every student needs. Good writing will be demanded throughout the high school and college years, but the need to write clearly does not end with school. Although many adults would not consider themselves professional writers, many of the careers by which they earn a living require the ability to communicate via the written word in one form or another.

Some written communications used in the workplace involve a combination of professional expertise and composition skills, such as is true for science or technical writing. Other forms of writing require the knowledge of certain formats, while some are subject to strict time constraints. All forms of writing necessitate the use of language which is easily understood by those who read it. Even writing on-the-job logs and anecdotal records demand clear language. Any writer must always write for his reader.

This book contains simulations of real-life situations in which competent writing is a part. Some of the simulations require only one or two days to complete. Others will occupy the plans for several days or weeks. Some basic writer's guidelines begin on page six with Tips for Good Writing. Other features of *Writing Simulations* include the following:

- ❑ Producing a television infomercial
- ❑ Publishing a literary magazine
- ❑ Writing online
- ❑ Writing in an emergency
- ❑ Historical writing
- ❑ Producing a television news magazine
- ❑ Writing in time: Essay exams
- ❑ Writing an autobiography
- ❑ Writing fiction: A class novel
- ❑ Writing a letter of complaint

In addition, activities are designed to increase vocabulary, to teach editing and proofreading skills, and to illustrate how to target student writing toward the reader. *Writing Simulations* can be used as the central resource for a whole language unit, or parts may be used on their own. This versatile unit gives specific writing strategies and is a must for the teacher wanting to teach a variety of writing applications.

Success with Simulations

The activities in *Writing Simulations* have been selected in order to get students involved with writing by actually simulating real-life situations in which people write as part of their jobs or for personal reasons.

Whether you are using a simulation as a unit in itself or as part of a larger unit, it is wise to establish procedures for storing and displaying the products resulting from it in a way which is consistent with the type of writing with which the unit deals.

Simulation Format

Each simulation begins with a lesson plan designed to help the teacher prepare and direct the necessary procedures and closes with valuable background information which connects the simulation with the actual work situation being studied and/or suggestions for follow-up activities to reinforce what has been learned with the simulation. The lesson plan for each simulation follows this format:

- ***Title of Simulation***
- ***Topic***
- ***Objective***
- ***Materials***
- ***Preparation***
- ***Procedure***
- ***Background and/or Follow-Up***

Storing Simulation Materials

You will want to save the components of a simulation activity, using a compact and organized system in order to have them for future use. Use labeled file folders, plastic sleeves, or large manila envelopes to sort pages to be duplicated, overhead transparencies, and small items; then, place the envelopes in file boxes or filing crates. Place a label or catalog of contents on the outside of the filing container so you can find it again easily.

Small pieces and samples of work to be saved for use as examples to future students can be laminated to better withstand being passed around by many hands.

Remember that you may have occasion to use individual simulation lessons at different times, depending on your class and plans. Having them quickly available as complete and individual units will be advantageous.

Now it's on to good writing!

Cooperative Learning Teams

For the novelist, freelancer, or poet who works alone at home or in an office with only a computer, typewriter, or pad and pencil, writing may be a solitary occupation. But even the solitary writer must work, sooner or later, with editors and others who take the initial written product and refine it for distribution to the public.

Today's students will someday find themselves in real-life educational and work situations where the emphasis will lie in their being able to work with others as part of a team. This is particularly true in the fields of social service and the media. It is true for police officers, medical personnel, and those who work for our newspapers, magazines, radio, and television. All of them write as part of their work, and all of them work together with their colleagues to produce a product or service.

Many workers and professionals must write under time constraints. A writer for a newspaper must meet deadlines and work with editors and other journalists. A police officer and medical personnel must turn in prompt, written reports and work closely with colleagues and the public. The press secretary of a public official must work very closely with that official so as to know how the official thinks in order to deal effectively with the public and the media.

Besides the anchors, reporters, and newscasters seen on the television screen, many people behind the scenes work in a television news room. Editors write and rewrite the lines to be read on the air. Directors and producers schedule the order in which news items will be broadcast and carefully ensure that each item goes on as scheduled. Other people provide technical support with great skill and energy. Nothing is left to chance, and everything is timed to the second.

Many other work situations are dependent on tight time constraints. Setting and adhering to a tight schedule requires people to cooperate with each other, along with the ability to be flexible in the interests of the entire enterprise.

For these reasons, *Writing Simulations* includes both independent and cooperative activities, with an emphasis on the cooperative. Heavy emphasis is also placed on the teacher modeling writing for students to give them precise strategies for writing for a specific purpose.

Four Basic Components of Cooperative Learning

1. *In cooperative learning, all group members need to work together to accomplish the task.*
2. *Cooperative learning groups should be heterogeneous.*
3. *Cooperative learning activities need to be designed so that each student contributes to the group, and individual group members can be assessed on their performance.*
4. *Cooperative learning teams need to know the social as well as the academic objectives of a lesson.*

Tips for Good Writing

The best writing is easy to read. The most creative ideas will be lost in writing which is complicated, flowery, or has too many adjectives and adverbs. Here are some tips for the student writer.

- ❑ **The most important words are nouns and verbs.** Nouns and verbs are the words needed to write or speak a sentence. Verbs are the power words which carry the flow of any form of written or spoken communication. Nouns and verbs do the work of writing. Use adjectives, adverbs, and helping words sparingly.

  Find specific nouns and verbs which paint a picture or tell a story. Use verbs which describe action. For example, instead of saying

  The girl ran home from school,

  say

  Jennie wasted no time and scurried down the street toward home.

  Jennie's name and the word *scurried* indicate a specific person and a specific action.

  The sentence shows us a certain girl acting in a certain way.

- ❑ **Use very few *-ing* words.** Write with strong verbs showing clear action. Instead of saying

  Dogs were barking,

  say

  The neighbor's poodle yipped, and then every dog for blocks around set up a howl.

  or

  Dozens of dogs sang a medley of yips, yelps, and yappings.

- ❑ **Write every day.** Set a daily goal of 100 words or 200 words—a goal you are certain you can reach. Write in a journal, a diary, wherever you wish, but write daily. With writing, and rewriting, practice does indeed make perfect.
- ❑ **Learn to type.** The computer can be a writer's best friend.
- ❑ **Keep a thesaurus and dictionary nearby and use them often.**
- ❑ **Rewrite! Rewrite! Rewrite!** Almost any sentence you can write in English can be written in many different ways. Learn to rewrite by habit to find the clearest way to say what it is you want to say.
- ❑ **Read! Read! Read!** Read anything and everything, but especially read the work of good writers. Reading will help you learn all the many possibilities of the language.

Writing Sentences

The sentence is the basic unit of thought. A sentence begins with a capital letter, and the most common kind of sentence—the declarative sentence—ends with a period. A capital letter at the beginning of a group of words and a period at the end of them are signals that a complete thought has been read. Without the capital letter and period, the reader might not be able to perceive when one thought has ended and another has begun.

But a capital letter at the beginning and a period at the end of a group of words are not the only things which make a group of words a sentence. The group of words *must contain at least one main subject and one main verb.* The subject and the verb go together to make the core, or kernel, of the sentence. The verb expresses an action or state of being, and the subject tells who or what is performing that action or state of being. The core, or kernel, of the sentence gives the reader the information needed to understand the thought by itself. Note how the following subjects and verbs go together in these sentences:

Two boys threw a football back and forth across the field.
subject *verb* *prepositional phrase*

Mr. Campbell drives his new automobile to work every day.
subject *verb* *prepositional phrase*

In the parade, a huge elephant clomped its way down the boulevard.
subject *verb* *prepositional phrase*

In these sentences, the sentence cores are "Two boys threw," "Mr. Campbell drives," and "a huge elephant clomped." Without these cores, the groups of words would not be sentences. They would be sentence fragments.

Identify the cores of these sentences by drawing one line under the subject and two lines under the verb.

- The people of the village were blessed with a large crop of corn.
- My dad took me and my brother to the movies.
- Bells rang in the church steeples the day the war ended.
- My neighbors celebrate Chanukah instead of Christmas.
- A good book is always one of my best friends.
- Happy days are here again.
- The wind howled around the house during the storm.

Sentence Fragments

When a group of words does not have a main subject and a main verb, it is a sentence fragment. It may begin with a capital letter. It may end with a period. But if it does not have a complete thought which comes from a subject and verb, it is not a complete sentence.

A sentence fragment is often a group of words called a dependent clause, because it needs to be attached to an independent clause (a complete sentence) to have meaning. Following are some examples of sentence fragments:

- Because he had not studied.
- Although we didn't have any money.
- Whenever the store is open.

When we read these groups of words, we are left wondering what comes next because they are not complete sentences. You can often spot a sentence fragment by the word, or words, with which it begins. If your "sentence" begins with one of these words or phrases, read the sentence again. It may be a sentence fragment if it is not attached to an independent clause.

after	though	as, as though, as if
because	before	even though
once	in order to	in order that
so that	than	since
though	unless	until
while	wherever	whomever, whoever
whether	whose	whenever
if	provided that	whereas

Also, if a group of words which is not a question begins with where, what, or when, it is probably a sentence fragment.

Draw a line under the sentence fragments.

- I did my homework after I got home.
- While John was in the living room watching television.
- Even though we'd gone to bed early and gotten plenty of sleep.
- I find a good book store wherever I go.
- Because Kay did well at school and got good grades.
- If you do not pass the test, you will not get a good grade in the class.

Writing Paragraphs

The sentence is the building block of writing, and the paragraph is what unifies and organizes sentences around a central idea or theme. Essays and reports must be written in paragraphs. Without the divisions between paragraphs, an essay or a long report would be difficult to read. With the division, the reader can take a little breather between ideas or find the place again after a pause.

The leading sentence alerts the reader to what will be the central idea of the paragraph. A good paragraph is composed of a central idea, sometimes called the main idea, and a variety of details to support the idea. The leading sentence is sometimes called the "topic sentence" because it tells the reader what the subject of the paragraph will be. The sentences which follow the first one supply details to show why the main idea is, or is not, true. Sometimes the sentences contain details which define or explain the main idea. Sometimes they offer concrete examples to back up the main idea. But they must hold the paragraph together.

Writers ask themselves questions which help them gather details. Sometimes they brainstorm ideas to come up with information which will form the body of a paragraph or essay. Sometimes they ask questions like these:

Who did it? Who is responsible? Who is involved?

What is the subject? What is the problem? What is the issue?

Where did this event take place?

When did it take place? When in my life? When in the lead character's life?

Why did it happen? What caused it? Why do I believe this?

How did it happen? What were the main ingredients?

Can I give an example?

Draw one line under the topic sentence in this paragraph and two lines under the sentences giving details.

Mr. Jameson, my teacher in sixth grade, was a great inspiration to me. He cared for his students, and he was always willing to stay after school to help me when I needed help. Math was hard for me, and if I didn't understand a problem in math, Mr. Jameson patiently explained it again to me in another way. Every day at lunch recess, before school, and after school there were students in his classroom getting extra help just as I was. He never yelled at the students or acted as though he didn't have time for them. One time I started crying in class because a test was so hard I thought I was going to fail it, and Mr. Jameson came over to me and put his hand on my shoulder. "You're doing just fine," he whispered and smiled. And I got a B on the test!

Edit These Sentences

Correct the errors in these sentences.

1. i didnt hear or notice that the bell had rung until mary tapped me on the should and pointed toward the school

2. come on she said were going to be late

3. we ran straight to class and their was mr miles the principle standing in front of the door

4. why are you late he asked us don't you know its important to get to class on time

5. im sorry i said i got so interested in the book i was reading i didnt here the bell i wont do it again i promise

6. i didnt want mr miles to call my parents because they would be really angry with me if i got in trouble i sweated out the rest of the afternoon

7. he kept his word though he didn't call my parents and i was never late for class again

8. that night i asked my dad why they worry so much about getting to class on time he said its to help kids get into the habit of being prompt because when we get out of school well have to get to work on time

9. im still not sure i understand what the big deal is about being on time but i know that i dont want to be late again

10. its embarrassing to be the last one through the door so everyone sees

Producing an Infomercial

SIMULATION #1

Topic

Writing and Producing an Infomercial for Television

Objective

Students will write and produce a one-minute infomercial for videotaped television. They will learn to write sparingly and to aim what they have to say to a specific audience. They will learn the importance of identifying the *who, what, where, when,* and *why* on which the success of an infomercial depends. They will act and film the infomercial, and after producing a finished product, they will evaluate their own success.

Materials

- overhead transparencies of pages 14, 15, and 17
- reproduce copies of pages 14, 16, 18, and 19
- overhead projector with marker
- videotape
- tape of two or three television commercials
- television monitor

Preparation

1. Reproduce pages 14, 16, 18, and 19.
2. Make overhead transparencies of pages 14, 15, and 17.
3. Prepare a short list of suggestions for items or services to "sell."
4. Arrange for use of videocamera.
5. Tape two or three commercials advertising products or services which students might be interested in for use in the classroom. These might include commercials for breakfast cereals, sneakers, sports equipment, etc.

Note to teacher: The best time or place to find an example of an infomercial which you can tape and show to the class might be either during a political campaign or on the business channel.

SIMULATION #1

Producing an Infomercial *(cont.)*

Procedure

1. Tell the students they are going to look closely at some television commercials because they are going to be making a special kind of commercial of their own, using procedures like the ones television stations use. Tell them that each commercial is usually only 30 seconds long and that commercials are produced for one reason only—to sell a product or service. Much information must be sent out to the viewer during that time limit.

2. Show the commercials one at a time. Ask the students to tell you what kinds of information are provided by each, and then list their answers on the board or chart paper. The answers should include the name of the product or service, where the product or service can be obtained, when it is available, and why they should want to purchase it.

3. Show one of the commercials again, this time stopping whenever the scene changes. Explain that each scene change is called a frame, and they are to be thinking in terms of writing "frames" of a commercial. Call on students to describe exactly what they see and what they hear in each frame and how all the frames go together to form one whole.

4. Explain that there is a special kind of commercial called an "infomercial." An infomercial is a commercial which operates under false pretenses. While we all know a commercial when we see one, we don't always recognize an infomercial at first, because it seems to be a news feature. It seems to offer only factual information, but just as a commercial is made to sell a product or service, so too is an infomercial. A typical infomercial consists of two people in a scene such as an office. One of them acts as a "teacher" or expert giving out useful information while the other acts as the "student" who is learning. A commercial can look like this too, but the big difference is that a commercial comes right out with the sales pitch whereas an infomercial sneaks it in under the guise of important information. Some political advertisements take the form of infomercials.

5. Distribute the Infomercial Objective Questionnaire (page 14). Explain that when an organization or business wants to have an infomercial made, their representative receives a questionnaire similar to this one to help the station and the business come to an agreement about what the infomercial is to accomplish. Infomercials are expensive to make, and no one wants to waste time planning infomercials with which no one is going to be happy. The students will use this form when planning their own infomercials.

6. Display the Video Storyboard transparency (page 15). Explain that this is the next step in planning an infomercial. It helps ensure that the video and the audio will match. Students will use this form. In their planning, they will have to include the name of the product, where and when it can be obtained, and why the viewer should purchase the product.

Producing an Infomercial *(cont.)*

Procedure *(cont.)*

7. Display the transparency of a "script" for an infomercial (page 17). The script contains the words and actions which have been planned, using the storyboard. It tells the actors and camera operator what to say and do. It plans the infomercial so the video portion and the audio portion will go together. Distribute blank storyboards and scripts (pages 16 and 18).

8. Divide the class into cooperative learning groups of about four or five. Each group is to plan an infomercial such as a business representative or politician would ask them to prepare. Its purpose is to sell a product, but it will be done in the form of a news feature. Students must decide on what product they want to sell, and then they are to complete the advertising questionnaire for that product.

9. Complete the storyboard with stick figures to represent the people in the infomercial. They may try several possibilities before deciding on one. After discussing which storyboard is best, the students should write a script based on the ideas on the storyboard. Remind them at this point of two things—to double-check whether they have included all the necessary information and to test whether they have used only one minute for the length of the infomercial. For a one-minute tape, they should not use more than two pages of script.

10. After they write the script, students are to produce the infomercials. Each group selects the members of the group to act, speak, and videotape or record the infomercial. They must rehearse the script to determine how long their script takes to cover. If they go over one minute, they must eliminate enough words to get the infomercial within time limits. If they are under one minute, they must "flesh out" their infomercial to fit exactly into one minute. They can have as many "takes" as they need to get the script right before recording it.

11. Finally, after writing and rehearsing, rewriting and redoing, the students are ready to record or televise their infomercial. One person in each group will videotape, one to three will act, one will direct and see that the actors and camera operator follow the script.

12. When all of the infomercials have been made, the class comes back together as a whole to view the infomercials. Students discuss how successful each is, and the students complete the Infomercial Evaluation (page 19).

Background

It is important for students to recognize that an infomercial exists for one purpose only: to sell something. An advertiser buys air time from a station to make money on the product being advertised. The writer uses words which will turn viewers into buyers.

When students learn exactly how and why an infomercial is made, they can be more discriminating viewers. Television is insidious in its ability to manipulate the public under the guise of informing them.

Infomercial Objective Questionnaire

Station Name ______________________________

Business Representative ______________________________

Business Name ______________________________

Business Address ______________________________

Phone/Fax Number ______________________________

Please double-check spelling and numbers for accuracy.

1. **Describe the product or service you represent.**

2. **Who is your competition?**

3. **How is your business different from others like yours?**

4. **Who are your present customers?**

5. **What customers do you want to reach?**

6. **What points are most essential in your infomercial?**

7. **What do you want the viewers of your infomercial to do?**

Video Storyboard

Project: Benefit Invest

Date: 3-16-97

Writer: MN

Video

Voice: Ladies and gentlemen,

Ms. Poppins

What is this I hear?

That is correct.

It's geared to what the client wants.

Incredible!

Just call!

Video Storyboard *(cont.)*

Project: ______________________________

Date: ______________________________

Writer: ______________________________

Video

Video Infomercial Script

CLIENT ____________________

TITLE ____________________

NAME ____________________

WRITER ____________________

DATE ____________________

ADDITIONAL INFORMATION ____________________

____

VIDEO	AUDIO
VOICE OF ANNOUNCER	LADIES AND GENTLEMEN: WE PROUDLY PRESENT MS. LILAH POPPINS, PRESIDENT OF BENEFIT INVESTMENT COMPANY
MS. POPPINS IS SHOWN WEARING A TAILORED SUIT AND LOOKING OBVIOUSLY WELL-OFF AND CONFIDENT.	HELLO, HOW ARE YOU?
ANNOUNCER	WHAT IS THIS I HEAR THAT BENEFIT INVESTMENT IS SHOWING ITS MEMBERS A TWENTY PERCENT RETURN ON THEIR MONEY?
MS. POPPINS	THAT IS CORRECT. MOST INVESTMENT COMPANIES DON'T SHOW THEIR CLIENTS HOW TO MAKE AS MUCH MONEY AS THEY COULD. WHEN WE INVEST THEIR MONEY, WE CAN POINT TO A HISTORY OF UNMATCHED PERFORMANCE, AND IT'S ALL GEARED TOWARD EXACTLY WHAT THE CLIENT WANTS.
ANNOUNCER	THAT IS INCREDIBLE! YOU MEAN TO SAY THAT IF I GIVE YOU $1,000, YOU WILL GIVE ME BACK $1,200—JUST LIKE THAT?
MS. POPPINS	THAT IS CORRECT. IT ISN'T MAGIC, AND IT DOESN'T INVOLVE SMOKE AND MIRRORS. WE USE COMMON, OLD-FASHIONED LOGIC TO PRODUCE SPECTACULAR RESULTS.
ANNOUNCER	AND HOW CAN WE GET INVOLVED?
MS. POPPINS	JUST CALL OUR OFFICES ANY TIME. OUR PEOPLE ARE HERE TO HELP.
GRAPHIC OF BENEFIT'S COMPANY LOGO	

Video Infomercial Script *(cont.)*

CLIENT ______________________________

TITLE ______________________________

NAME ______________________________

WRITER ______________________________

DATE ______________________________

ADDITIONAL INFORMATION ______________________________

____

VIDEO	AUDIO

Infomercial Evaluation

After the infomercial has been produced, answer these questions about how successful it is. Discuss your answers with the rest of the class.

1. Does this infomercial tell **what** is being sold?

   Does this infomercial tell **where** to find the product or service?

   Does this infomercial tell **when** you can find it?

   Does this infomercial tell you **why** you should want it?

   Does this infomercial tell you **how** you can get it?

2. Does this infomercial look or sound like an ordinary commercial?

   Explain:

3. Does this infomercial make the product or service sound as though it is doing the customer a favor?

   Explain:

4. Does this infomercial seem to inform the viewer of essential information?

   Explain:

5. Is this infomercial more or less effective than a commercial would be?

   Explain:

6. On a scale of 1 to 6, with 6 being very effective and 1 being not so effective, rank this infomercial as to its effectiveness.

SIMULATION #2

Publishing a Literary Magazine

Topic

Writing and Publishing a Class Literary Magazine

> **Note to teacher:** This simulation involves the production of many pieces of literature and will require a fair amount of time. Allow sufficient number of weeks for the simulation to be completed. Class level will dictate whether all or only some of the activities will be included. For example, lower levels may not be able to complete the sonnets.

Objective

Students will write and publish a class literary magazine which contains a variety of writing purposes and styles and which also reflects the "personality" of the individual classroom.

Materials

- transparencies of pages 24, 25, 26, 27, 28, 29, 30, 31, and 32
- copies of pages 24, 25, 26, 27, 28, 29, 30, 31, and 32
- paper, pencils, and pens
- selection of magazines
- overhead projector and marker
- access to computer and photocopy machine

Preparation

1. Make transparencies of pages 24, 25, 26, 27, 28, 30, 31, and 32
2. Make reproduced copies of pages 24, 25, 26, 27, 28, 29, 30, 31, and 32
3. Gather copies of magazines which feature stories, poems, essays, and book reviews to show the students.
4. Obtain an overhead projector and marker.
5. Arrange for use of a computer and photocopy machine.

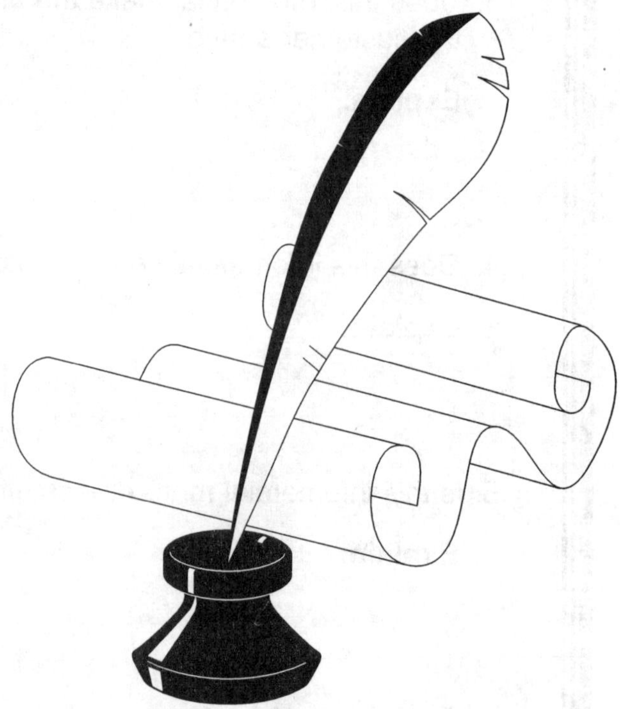

Publishing a Literary Magazine *(cont.)*

SIMULATION #2

Procedure

1. Tell the students they are going to publish a literary magazine. Explain that a literary magazine contains stories, poems, essays, and book reviews, and that many famous writers got their starts as published writers by being published in literary magazines.
2. Show the sample magazines you have brought to class. Ask the students what general differences there are among these magazines and other magazines they have read. How might the ads in a literary magazine be different from those in another kind of magazine? Discuss how the content and style included in a magazine give each magazine its own "personality." What kinds of paper are used? What kinds of covers? Help the students discern the most obvious differences among the publications. Tell them that writers of a literary magazine write for their readers—other people who like to read stories, essays, and poetry. The students will be writing poetry first.
3. Place the transparency Writing Poetry (page 24) on the overhead projector and distribute copies. Explain that the students are going to begin their magazine by exploring and writing different kinds of poetry. Read the paper together and discuss the properties of poetry. Discuss *imagery, similes, metaphors, rhythm, rhyme,* and *point of view*. Ascertain the students' grasp of these literary concepts by having them give examples. If student grasp is uncertain, complete one or more activities designed to teach the concepts before proceeding with this simulation. Reading examples of poetry containing these literary devices will be beneficial to the students. For example, James Weldon Johnson's poem "The Creation," available in many anthologies of children's literature, can be used to demonstrate all the properties of poetry, as well as all the literary terms except rhyme. It is especially good for teaching about imagery and rhythm.
4. Distribute Writing Ballads (page 25) and place the transparency on the overhead projector. Tell students that the ballad is one of the oldest forms of poetry in the English language. Centuries before the invention of radio, television, and the printing press, troubadours and minstrels of the Middle Ages went from town to town singing ballads of their own making which told news and gossip from other towns. Ballads are still being written today. Many of today's popular country-western songs are ballads—that is, songs which can be identified by the stories they tell. Ask students whether any of them can name a country-western song which tells a story.
5. Read the "Ballad of Sir Patrick Spens" to the class as the students read silently along with you. Emphasize the rhythm and rhyme of the ballad and the story it tells. Have students read the poem aloud as a choral reading. Stress that a ballad is written to be said or sung aloud, and that sometimes the pronunciation of the words is slightly altered in the reading in order to maintain the rhythm and rhyme. Tell them they are going to be writing ballads.

SIMULATION #2

Publishing a Literary Magazine *(cont.)*

Procedure (cont.)

6. Divide the class into cooperative learning groups. Assign each group the task of writing a ballad. Remind them their ballad must tell a story and have a simple rhyme scheme. They can use a story in the news, or they could use a story from childhood (such as *The Three Little Pigs*) as the basis for their ballad. When the ballads are finished, have a spokesperson for each group read the ballad that group has written. Discuss how successful the ballads have been. Collect samples of class ballads to be saved for inclusion in the class literary magazine.
7. Distribute Writing Limericks (page 26), and place the transparency on the overhead projector. Tell the students limericks are one of the most lighthearted and amusing kinds of poetry. Some of them are called nonsense poems because they do not always make much sense. Read the limericks together, and then break into cooperative learning groups. The learning groups are to write several limericks of their own. When the students return as a class, read some of the limericks they have written. Collect samples of limericks to be saved for inclusion in the literary magazine.
8. Distribute Writing Sonnets (pages 27 and 28) and place the transparency for page 27 on the overhead projector. This is the most complex poetry they will be studying. Read the information on page 27 together and discuss how education has changed during the past 500 years. In Shakespeare's time, when these sonnets were written, learning to read Ancient Greek and Latin and writing poetry were some of the most important components of education. Of course, during that time only the wealthy and privileged were able to get an education. Most young people began working at some menial job at which they would spend their lives toiling. They also did not live very long. Many died at a very young age. Still, these sonnets are considered by most people to be some of the most beautiful words ever written in English. Read the sonnets on page 28 together. Determine that the students understand the rhyme scheme of the sonnet.
9. Divide the class into cooperative learning groups. Assign each group the task of writing a sonnet. When sonnets have been written, bring students back together as a class. Read their sonnets aloud and discuss them. Collect samples of sonnets to be saved for inclusion in the literary magazine.
10. Distribute Poetry Starters (page 29). Tell students the poems they write for this part of the simulation will be personal. Stress that there is no "right" or "wrong" way for them to write these poems, and it is only when reading a poem that its poetic merit can be determined. Allow them to choose two or three different types of poems and write some of their own. Allow those who wish to do so to share their poems. Collect samples of free verse to be saved for inclusion in the literary magazine.

Publishing a Literary Magazine *(cont.)*

Procedure (cont.)

11. Distribute Writing Short Stories (page 30), and display the transparency on the overhead. Read the information together. Discuss some short stories the students have read in class, and identify how the elements of a short story fit the stories they have read. Tell them they will use the outline on the page to plan their own stories. Provide writing time. Review good editing skills (page 10). Save samples of edited stories for inclusion in the literary magazine.
12. Save samples of essays written in Simulation #3 Writing in Time (page 33) to be included in the literary magazine.
13. Distribute Reviewing Fiction (page 31). Assign book reviews to interested students. Save samples of book reviews to be included in the magazine.
14. Choose personnel for the magazine (page 32). Editors should be students who are self-directing and have the ability to organize and focus others. All class members must have definite roles to fill. More than one student can be co-editor as long as those two are able to work well together.
15. Set a time limit for the duration of putting the magazine together. Dedicate a certain amount of time each day to working on the magazine.
16. When all submissions have been collected and edited, it is time to "lay out" the magazine so the entries fit together reasonably well, filling in the blank spaces with drawings or very short items. Because some students will be more motivated in writing, encourage individual submissions as well as group ones. Possibilities for fillers include jokes and riddles. Word puzzles or trivia quizzes are also possibilities. All submissions to the magazine should be okayed by the teacher, who is ultimately responsible for its production and its quality.
17. The rest is the easy part! Reproduce all pages on the copy machine. Set up a team to collate the pages and fasten them together. You're in print!

Background

The students may not have seen a magazine which is devoted solely to writing and publishing of stories, poems, and essays. Writing and publishing a class literary magazine enables the students to explore many different writing genres and then have the thrill of seeing their own creations "in print." The incentive to write is high when the students know their work will be published.

Putting the magazine together will give students ownership in a collection of work which they create and on which they collaborate, as well as giving them experience in writing different genres. They will have a product of their own of which they can be truly proud.

Writing Poetry

What exactly is a poem—some lines that rhyme? Lines that fit into a certain form or shape? Condensed speech which says as much between the lines as it does within them? Yes and no. A poem can rhyme, but it may not. A poem might fit a certain form or shape, but the form or shape could be either a traditional one or one the poet creates for just one poem. And most poems say more than just the words within them. They use language well.

There are as many kinds and styles of poems as there are poets to write them. The poetry forms described in detail in this simulation are the more formal, traditional ones like ballads, sonnets, and limericks. But other kinds of poetry are also acceptable in a literary magazine. Some suggestions as to how to generate some other kinds of poetry are on page 29.

What do good poems have in common? Whatever the form of poetry, most poems share certain properties. They combine music and idea, sound and sense, feeling and meaning. All of these must work together to make a poem one we want to read again and again. To create all these properties in a poem, a poet uses *imagery*. He puts words together in such a way as to create mental pictures in the reader's head. The use of *similes*, in which two things are compared to each other using the words *like* or *as* is one kind of imagery. The use of *metaphors*, in which two things are compared to each other as though they were the same, is another kind of imagery.

A poet uses sound. He may use soft sounds, sounds almost hushed, to create one kind of feeling, and then use harsh sounds, sounds which boom off the page, to create another kind of feeling. He may use staccato sounds to create a feeling of movement or playfulness. And he combines the sounds and imagery with rhythm. The rhythm in some poems is fast and jerky. In others it is slow and dreamy. Sometimes the rhythm contributes to the feeling of the poem.

Some poems rhyme. Rhyme can dictate the structure of a poem, as it does in the limerick and the sonnet. Sometimes rhyme in a poem is pleasant to hear, but at other times it gets in the way of the poem's meaning. When the lines of a poem rhyme at the ends of the lines, it is called *external rhyme*. But some rhymes are within the lines, and this kind of rhyme is called *internal rhyme*.

Poems also reflect point of view. If the poem is very personal, it might be written in the first person—that is, from the "I" point of view. If it is a love poem, it would probably be written in the second person to you. If the poet wants to tell the poem from a distance, he would write it in the third person.

Read some of the poems in this simulation—try them on for size. What kind fits you best?

Writing Ballads

Ballads and songs have been composed for hundreds of years—since before most people could read and write. They were told and sung orally to people across the countryside of England, often as a way of spreading news about unusual things that happened. This ballad is about a ship which sank off the coast of Scotland and the brave man who captained it.

Ballad of Sir Patrick Spens

The king sits in Dumferline town,
Drinking the blood-red wine:
"O where will I get a skeely skipper
To sail this new ship of mine?"

O up and spake an eldern knight,
Sate at the king's right knee—
"Sir Patrick Spens is the best sailor
That ever sailed the sea."

Our king has written a broad letter,
And sealed it with his hand,
And sent it to Sir Patrick Spens
Was walking on the strand.

The first word that Sir Patrick read,
So loud, loud laughed he;
The next word that Sir Patrick read,
The tear blinded his ee.

"O who is this has done this deed,
And told the king o' me,
To send us out, this time o' year,
To sail upon the sea?

"Make ready, make ready, my merry men,
Our good ship sails the morn."
"Now ever alack, my master dear,
I fear a deadly storm!

"I saw the new moon, late yestreen,
With the auld moon in her arm;
And if we gang to sea, master,
I fear we'll come to harm."

They had not sailed a league, a league,
A league but barely three,
when the lift grew dark, and the wind blew loud,
And gurly grew the sea.

O loth, loth were our good Scots lords
To wet their cork-heeled shoon!
But lang ere a' the play was play'd
They wet their hats aboon.

O long, long may the ladies sit,
With their fans into their hand
Before they see Sir Patrick Spens
Come sailing to the strand!

And long, long may the maidens sit,
Wi' the goud combs in their hair,
All waiting for their own dear loves—
For them they'll see no mair.

Half owre, half owre to Aberdour
Tis fifty fathoms deep,
And there lies good Sir Patrick Spens,
With the Scots lords at his feet.

Writing Limericks

Limericks are formal poems in the sense that they follow a prescribed rhyme scheme and rhythm, but unlike sonnets which are often very serious, limericks are full of fun. They are an example of how rhyming can structure a poem. Many limericks begin with "There was an old man who . . ." or "There was an old woman who . . . ." A famed master at writing limericks and other nonsense poems was Edward Lear. Here are a few examples of his limericks.

There was an Old Man in a tree,
Whose whiskers were lovely to see;
But the birds of the air pluck'd them perfectly bare,
To make themselves nests in that tree.

There is a young lady, whose nose,
Continually prospers and grows;
When it grew out of sight, she exclaimed in a fright,
"Oh! Farewell to the end of my nose!"

There was an Old Man on whose nose
Most birds of the air could repose;
But they all flew away at the closing of day,
Which relieved that Old Man and his nose.

There was a Young Lady of Norway,
Who casually sat in a doorway;
When the door squeezed her flat, she exclaimed, "What of that?"
This courageous Young Lady of Norway.

There was an old man on the Border,
Who lived in the utmost disorder;
He danced with the cat, and made tea in his hat,
Which vexed all the folks on the Border.

There was an Old Man who said, "Hush!
I perceive a young bird in this bush!"
When they said, "Is it small?" he replied, "Not at all;
It is four times as big as the bush!"

There was an old man, who when little
Fell casually into a kettle;
But, growing too stout, he could never get out,
So he passed all his life in that kettle.

There was an old person of Ware,
Who rode on the back of a bear;
When they ask'd "Does it trot?" he said "Certainly not!
He's a Moppsikon Floppsikon bear!"

Do you get the idea of how limericks work? Try some of your own!

Writing Sonnets

Until the last century, the educated person was expected not only to memorize and recite classical poetry but also to write poetry. Indeed, a person who could not write poetry was considered barely literate. A favorite traditional kind of poem written by Shakespeare and most classical poets is the *sonnet.*

Shakespeare wrote 154 sonnets which are considered some of the English speaking world's most beautiful lines. When the term *Elizabethan Sonnet* is used, it refers to sonnets constructed like those Shakespeare wrote. Most sonnets consisted of single, fourteen-line poems, but sometimes Elizabethan poets wrote entire narratives in sonnet form.

A sonnet follows a set of rules.

1. There are 14 lines all together in a sonnet.
   - A. There are three sets of four lines called *quatrains*.
   - B. There are two lines at the end called a *couplet*.
2. Each line contains 10 syllables with every other syllable accented, usually beginning with the second syllable in each line.

   Example: *When in the chronicle of wasted time*

3. The sonnet has a formal *rhyme scheme* which is as follows:

   abab

   cdcd

   efef

   gg

   In this rhyme scheme the "a's" rhyme with each other, the "b's" rhyme with each other, and so forth.

4. The sonnet also has a *thematic structure*. Usually, the first two quatrains set up a problem, the third quatrain begins to answer the problem, and the ending couplet tries to solve the problem.

On the following page are two Shakespearean sonnets with the quatrains, couplets, and rhyme schemes identified for you on the first one. Can you identify the quatrains, couplets, and rhyme scheme of the second sonnet?

Challenge: What are the problems and solutions of these sonnets?

Writing Sonnets *(cont.)*

5

quatrain	*Those hours that with gentle work did frame*	*a*
	The lovely gaze where every eye doth dwell	*b*
	Will play the tyrants to the very same	*a*
	And that unfair which fairly doth excel.	*b*
quatrain	*For never-resting time leads summer on*	*c*
	To hideous winter and confounds him there,	*d*
	Sap checked with frost and lusty leaves quite gone,	*c*
	Beauty o'ersnowed and bareness everywhere.	*d*
quatrain	*Then, were not summer's distillation left,*	*e*
	A liquid prisoner pent in walls of glass,	*f*
	Beauty's effect with beauty were bereft,	*e*
	Nor it, nor no remembrance what it was.	*f*
couplet	*But flowers distilled, though they with winter meet,*	*g*
	Lose but their show. Their substance still lives sweet.	*g*

116

Let me not to the marriage of true minds
Admit impediments. Love is not love
Which alters when it alteration finds,
Or bends with the remover to remove.
Oh no! It is an ever-fixed mark
That looks on tempests and is never shaken.
It is the star to every wandering bark,
Whose worth's unknown, although his height be taken.
Love's not Time's fool, though rosy lips and cheeks
Within his bending sickle's compass come.
Love alters not with his brief hours and weeks,
But bears it out even to the edge of doom.
If this be error and upon me proved,
I never writ, nor no man ever loved.

Poetry Starters

Poems can be written in any shape or form, with any rhythm, with or without rhyme. Poems written without any prescribed structure are called *free verse*. Here are some ideas you can try out for your own free verse.

- ❑ **Write an "I" poem:** Write a poem in which every line begins with "I." What do you love? What do you hate? What do you dream of? What do you long for? How do you feel? What special time do you remember? What lies ahead? Write it into a poem.
- ❑ **Write a "You" poem:** This is a poem you write to someone who is significant in your life. Sometimes a "you" poem is a love poem but not always. It could be to the person with whom you have the perfect friendship, to a sister or brother, to a parent or a teacher. It could even be to someone you have never met but would like to meet or to someone in history, someone you've seen in a photograph or painting.
- ❑ **Write a poem about your favorite things.**
- ❑ **Write a poem about something you feel deeply.** What are you afraid of? What do you love most? What gives you hope? How do you feel about having lost someone who meant a lot to you? What do you want most from life? What dreams do you have? How do you want to accomplish your dreams?
- ❑ **Write a descriptive poem.** Describe your best friend, your pet, your room, your neighborhood, your country, or your life.
- ❑ **Write about something in nature.** The whole world is your subject! Write a poem about trees, flowers, plants, clouds, a spring storm, snow, a bubbling brook or a rushing river, a covey of quail skittering across the lawn on a cloudy day, the roar of the ocean, the hush of a snowfall, the pounding of hail on the roof and the flash of lightning down through the sky, or the pattern of frost on the window.
- ❑ **Write about what makes you laugh.** As you have seen with limericks, poems don't have to be serious. They can be as full of fun as you are!

You can write a poem about absolutely ANYTHING!

Writing Short Stories

A story is planned by its author. It doesn't just flow out of the tips of the writer's fingers. Most writers outline their stories before they actually begin writing. An author takes care to include all the major elements of a short story. Those elements are *setting, characters,* and *plot.*

- **Setting** is where and when the story happens.
- **Characters** are the people or animals the story is about.
- **Plot** is what happens in the story.

The reader needs to know right away who the story is about and what the setting is. After the setting is established and the characters are introduced, the events in a story can follow, one after the other, until the story ends. To plan a short story, answer these questions:

Where and **when** will my story take place? ____________________

____

Who will my story be about? ____________________

What does my main character want? ____________________

____

What will happen to prevent my character from getting what he or she wants?

Event 1 ____________________

____

Event 2 ____________________

____

Event 3 ____________________

____

How will my main character solve his/her problem? ____________________

____

____

____

When you have answered all these questions, you are well on your way to writing your short story!

Reviewing Fiction

A book review is not a book report that a student has to do in order to get a good grade. Book reviewers read many books because they love to read, and they love to tell people about what they read. Sometimes they write about how much they liked certain books. Sometimes they write about how much they didn't like others. They always tell why. And they get a lot of attention from others who also like to read.

When writing a book review, you write for your reader, in this case someone who likes to read books, and you need to have a "hook," a beginning which grabs the interest of the reader. The hook can be a quotation from the book being reviewed, a statement about one of the characters in the book, or an analogy in which you compare some aspect of this book with something else. Your hook is limited only by your imagination and grasp of the book you are reviewing.

After grabbing your reader's attention, you need to keep his attention by writing clearly and following the guidelines of writing well (see Tips for Good Writing, page 6). Use this checklist as a guide to ensure that you include all the necessary information your review needs to contain.

Checklist

——**Title**

——**Author**

——**Describe the main character.**
What is there about this person which makes the reader care about him or her? It's hard to like a book peopled with unlikable characters, especially if the main character is difficult to like.

——**Describe the problem which the main character faces.**
What does the character want? What is preventing him or her from getting what is wanted? Is there something wrong with the character which is preventing him or her from getting what is wanted, or do the problems lie outside the character?

——**Describe one thing the character does to solve the problem.**
Is the action successful? Why or why not?

——**Evaluate the book.**
Tell why you did, or did not, like it.
Would you recommend this book to others? Why?

——**Do NOT tell how the story ends!**

Good reading!

Magazine Personnel

Editor in Chief ______________________________

Assistant Editor ______________________________

Poetry Editor ______________________________

Assistant Poetry Editor ______________________________

Short Story Editor ______________________________

Assistant Short Story Editor ______________________________

Book Reviewer ______________________________

Assistant Book Reviewer ______________________________

Essay Editor ______________________________

Assistant Essay Editor ______________________________

Art Director ______________________________

Assistant Art Director ______________________________

Copy Editors ______________________________

____

____

____

Cover Editor ______________________________

Writing in Time: Essay Exams

SIMULATION #3

Topic

Writing on a Specific Subject in a Limited Amount of Time

Objective

Students will write essays on a specific subject chosen by the teacher and will do it in the amount of time specified. They will plan their essays as directed, write them, and proofread them successfully.

Materials and Equipment

- transparencies of pages 36–40, 42
- reproduced copies of pages 36–42
- overhead projector and marker
- wall chart of Ten Steps Toward Writing a Good Essay, page 36
- paper
- scratch paper
- pencils, pens
- computer with word processor and/or typewriter

> **Note to teacher:** This simulation can be used without transparencies, but modeling is easier with an overhead than without. The overhead projection makes it possible for the teacher to maintain consistent eye contact with the students as they "write" an essay together and takes less time than having to turn back and forth to the chalkboard.

Preparation

1. Make transparencies of pages 36–40, and 42.
2. Reproduce copies of pages 36–42.
3. Make a wall chart of page 36 for students' future reference.
4. Arrange for use of an overhead projector.

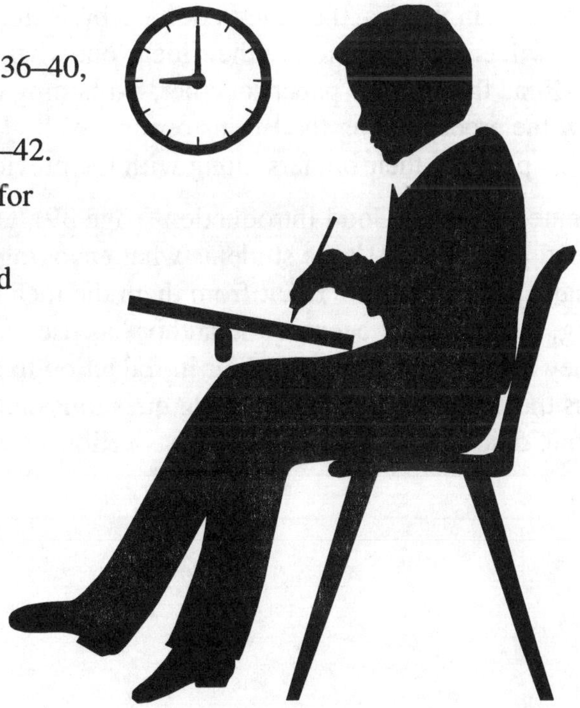

Writing in Time: Essay Exams *(cont.)*

Procedure

1. Inform students they are going to learn how to write in-class essays under time limits. Explain that essay exams are common forms of tests and exams they will have to take many times in high school and college, and this simulation will help them learn the skill of writing within time limits on a topic chosen by the teacher.
2. Distribute Ten Steps Toward Writing a Good Essay and indicate the wall chart. Inform students that this wall chart will remain on the wall throughout the school year and that they must keep the reproduced copy handy in their binders. Stress the first step—Have a plan. Learning and following the plan provided by this chart will help them systemize their writing of essay exams. It also will provide them with a guide to use when writing out-of-class essay assignments. Writing essay exams and writing out-of-class essays require the same basic skills and processes. Their difference lies only in the amount of time taken.
3. Read through the list of steps on the chart after telling the students they will soon be re-reading these one at a time and discussing their meanings more in depth. If they do not understand the steps at this point, remind them that their questions will probably be answered as they re-read and discuss the steps together.
4. Go back to step 2, Identify Key Words and What They Mean and distribute copies of page 37. Display the transparency and refer to it as the students refer to their copies. Explain that essay exams usually follow one of several patterns and that they need to learn the key words often used in essay questions. This will enable them to know exactly what the question is which they will have to answer. This is an important step. Discuss the key words until you are satisfied the students have good grasp of their meanings. Tell them to keep this chart in their binders for future reference.
5. Distribute copies of Brainstorming (page 38) and Brainstorming Web (page 95), and display the transparency on the overhead. Inform students that while they have brainstormed in groups, they may not have brainstormed independently before. This process will enable them to lay their ideas out where they can see them as they plan an essay. Read through the paper together, explaining clustering if it is a new to them. Review the process using the Brainstorming Web. Discuss freewriting. Tell them to keep this paper in their binders along with the previous two papers.
6. Distribute Writing a Good Introduction (page 39), and display the transparency on the overhead projector. Ask the students what encourages them to keep on reading a book they have just picked up. Elicit from them the idea that when they decide to continue reading, it is probably because the author has used a "hook" to grab their interest and that they need to use a hook in their introduction to an essay in the same way. Read and discuss the different ideas about using questions, anecdotes, analogies, quotations, dialogue, description, and provocative assertions.

Writing in Time: Essay Exams *(cont.)*

Procedure (cont.)

7. Display Putting Your Essay Together (page 40), and distribute copies. This is the fifth and final paper in this simulation which you expect students to keep in their binders for future reference. Read the paper together. Inform students this is the most common structure for an essay to take, and once they learn it, it will become an automatic response when they are about to write an essay.
8. When the students have asked all their questions and seem comfortable with what is expected of them, tell them you are going to give them a chance to reinforce what they have discussed with an "open-book" quiz (page 41) in which they look for answers in the five pages just discussed. Divide them into cooperative learning groups to take the quiz.
9. Have students come back from groups to a full class. Display Putting Your Essay Together (page 40), and choose one of the essay questions for a group essay. Working through the steps on Writing a Good Essay, compose a class essay on the overhead with input from the students. Ask students to identify a step for each part of the essay. This will probably take an entire class period to complete. Spend considerable time on the final step—proofreading—because this may be the students' first experience with editing a paper. Elicit from the students the rules for changes made and discuss them.

   Note: This process can be successfully completed on computers if there is access to computers for each one or two students. It will give them excellent practice in using a word processor.
10. After all editing of the class essay has been completed, have students rewrite the paper and turn it in.
11. Distribute Practice Essay Questions (page 42). Explain that this is the form that essay exams take to get into some colleges and universities, and that the students are to complete an in-class essay for one of them. Assign one of the questions. Allow them to use their copies of pages 36 through 40 for reference as they complete their essays. At the conclusion of the essays, discuss with the class any problems they had completing the essay. Tell them they will return to this activity periodically during the year as reinforcement.

Follow-Up

Periodically during the remainder of the school year, assign an essay question similar to the ones the students have done in this simulation. The reinforcement will help them master the skill of writing essay exams.

Background

As the general economy becomes more and more technological, the need for writing and proofreading skills becomes greater. Students need to become accustomed to writing as they have in this simulation so that they can do it almost on autopilot.

Ten Steps Toward Writing a Good Essay

- **Have a plan.** You need to organize your information before you begin writing.
- **Identify key words in your question or topic.** You want to make certain you are answering the question which has been asked, not a different question.
- **Brainstorm.** Using key words as clues, brainstorming helps you to generate and organize your ideas.
- **Outline the ideas from brainstorming.** Put your ideas into the order you wish your essay to have.
- **Begin writing.**
- **Write a first paragraph which states the central idea of your essay.**
- **Have a main idea for each paragraph.** Each paragraph should reinforce the central idea of the essay.
- **Do not write one-sentence or one-page paragraphs.** While you want to vary the types and lengths of sentences you use, your paragraph size should be relatively consistent.
- **Write a conclusion and then check your essay.** Have you answered the question? Have you supported your central idea?
- **Proofread.** Read your essay carefully and correct any errors in grammar, spelling, and punctuation.

Key Words and What They Mean

Analyze

When you *analyze* something, you break it into parts to find how the parts are related to each other. This helps you to learn why events happened as they did or why you believe the way you do.

When you analyze, you discuss cause and effect, explain your opinions or interpretations, and reveal facts and truths.

These key words are similar to analyze: *evaluate, examine, explain.*

Argue or Support

To *argue* or *support* means for you to take a stand for or against an issue. Then you must give evidence and reasons why you feel the way you do.

These key words are similar to argue or support: *justify, defend.*

Describe

To *describe* means to use carefully selected details to recreate an issue or a thing so that your reader can understand it. You may need to tell a story about what happened.

These key words are similar to describe: *narrate, relate, tell about, depict, portray.*

Discuss

When you *discuss*, you tell about a subject from more than one perspective. You may point out several different aspects of the subject, or you may talk about several different points.

These key words are similar to discuss: *compare, contrast.*

Brainstorming

Brainstorming is a way of generating and developing ideas by associating them with other ideas. It's a way of discovering what you want to say when you don't know already what that is. Brainstorming allows one idea to lead to another. When you brainstorm, you put down thoughts and ideas as they come to you. There are no good or bad ideas when you're brainstorming, as long as you stick to the main idea.

You and the other members of a group may have been asked to do this before. Your teacher may have told you to go into cooperative learning groups and brainstorm ideas for a story, for a class party, or for the possible answers to a question. In this way, you and your group have uncovered everyone's ideas in order to make a decision. But you don't need to be in a group to brainstorm. You can use it when you are writing a report or taking an essay exam.

Here are some tips about how to use brainstorming when you are taking an essay exam.

Brainstorming for Essays

- ❑ **Use key words as clues for ideas.**

  Your exam question will give you clues about how to frame your essay response. Read the question carefully and then ask yourself, "What key words does this question give me?" Underline them. The key words will tell you whether to analyze, argue or support, describe, or discuss your ideas.

  Next ask yourself, "Exactly what does the question ask me to analyze, argue or support, describe, or discuss?" Underline the words which answer this question.

- ❑ **Use clustering to "see" what you have to say.**

  Use the structure of the Brainstorming Web (page 95) to picture the ideas which the underlined words bring to mind. This action allows you to gather "clusters" of related ideas to use when you write the essay.

- ❑ **Freewrite and then analyze what you have written.**

  Sometimes you feel you have absolutely nothing to write about. Freewriting can be a solution to this problem. The physical process of sitting down and writing what comes to mind may start your ideas flowing. You will have to organize your ideas later, but writing, even though you think you have nothing to say, can show you that you do have something to say, after all, and that your ideas are the stuff of which an essay answer is made.

Writing a Good Introduction

When you write, you must always remember to write for your reader. And when you write for your reader, you need to have a "hook." A hook is something which intrigues the reader, creates a puzzle, or in some way gives the beginning some style, originality, or significance. In an essay exam, there are several techniques you can use to accomplish this, including those which appear below.

Introduction "Hooks"

- ❑ **Question:** Using a question is the easiest hook to use for an essay exam. A question at the beginning of an essay gives it a sense of mystery and suspense and allows the reader to feel he or she is participating in the answer. Sometimes a series of questions is effective, as well. On the topic of what makes a good teacher, for example, the essay might begin like this:

  > *Do you remember the best teacher you ever had? What was there about that person that made him (or her) so good? Was it the way that teacher looked? Was it the way that teacher ran the class? Or was it what that teacher said that made him or her so memorable?*

  The rest of the introductory paragraph would be spent setting out the central idea of the essay—what makes a good teacher.

- ❑ **Anecdote:** Begin your essay with a short, revealing or humorous narrative that falls within the central idea of the essay. It must be short enough to fit within the paragraph with enough room left to set forth your central idea.

- ❑ **Analogy:** In an analogy, you compare your subject to something unrelated, but common, in order to reveal some aspect of the subject. You can do this by beginning with your subject, adding the phrase "is like," and completing the sentence. It is possible to draw out the comparison for almost the entire paragraph.

- ❑ **Quotation or Dialogue:** Use a quotation from a known authority to give your essay background and prestige right from the start.

- ❑ **Description:** Use vivid details to grab the reader's attention.

- ❑ **Provocative Assertion:** Challenge your reader's thinking. For example, state an "obvious" idea with which "everyone" agrees and then contradict it as is done here:

  > *All students deserve to get "A's" on their report cards. Right? Wrong! Grades must be based on the quality of the work a student does, not just the fact that he makes it to class every day!*

Putting Your Essay Together

Once you know how to identify the key words in an essay question, how to brainstorm your ideas, and how to organize them into a good paragraph, you are ready to write an entire essay with several paragraphs. You must plan your writing so you have a sense of how your essay will look when it is finished.

A good essay begins with an introductory paragraph which contains a central idea, develops the central idea through several paragraphs called "body paragraphs," and ends with a concluding paragraph. The body paragraphs support and explain the central idea of the essay, and the concluding paragraph draws matters to a close, offers a summary or prediction, and restates the central idea.

The structure of a five-paragraph essay will look like this:

Paragraph 1.	**Introduction**
Paragraph 2.	**Develops topic A**
Paragraph 3.	**Develops topic B**
Paragraph 4.	**Develops topic C**
Paragraph 5.	**Conclusion**

Not all essays will have five paragraphs. Some will have fewer than five. Some will have more than five. The same general plan should be followed for your essay, whatever the number of paragraphs it contains. Topics A, B, and C form the "body" of this essay.

Essay Practice

Choose one of the following essay questions, and write an essay with the structure above. First, identify your key words.

1. Analyze the qualities of a good teacher. What does a good teacher do? What could a poor teacher do to improve? Use specific examples to support your central idea and reach a conclusion based on what you have observed.
2. Write an essay in which you argue for or against the way in which students in your school are graded. Are students graded fairly? On what do you base your opinion? Use specific examples and reach a conclusion based on what you have experienced.
3. Discuss the effect of television violence on children. Is television violence harmful? Explain. Use specific examples to support your opinion and reach a conclusion based on what you have observed.

Quiz

Write answers to the following questions.

1. The words *analyze, argue, support, describe,* and *discuss* are called ____________________.
2. Other words for *analyze* are ____________________.
3. Other words for *support* are ____________________.
4. Other words for *describe* are ____________________.
5. Other words for *discuss* are ____________________.
6. The first step in brainstorming is ____________________.
7. Freewriting is ____________________.
8. Define "hook." ____________________

   ____

   ____

   ____

9. Show the structure of a five-paragraph essay:

   ____

   ____

   ____

   ____

   ____

   ____

   ____

10. What is the final step in writing a good essay? ____________________

    ____

    ____

    ____

    ____

Practice Essay Questions

You will have 10 minutes to read and think about one of the following topics. You may make notes or outlines on scratch paper. At the end of 10 minutes, you will have 30 minutes to write your essay. Allow yourself at least five minutes to edit and proofread. Dictionaries may be used in this part of the examination.

✦ ✦ ✦

A. It has been suggested that true happiness lies in having the freedom to be the person you want to be. Many people spend large amounts of their time doing what they think others expect of them, rather than becoming who they really wish to be inside. One person may become a lawyer because his father is a lawyer. Another might become an engineer like her mother, rather than going into medicine as she wants to do, thus ending up frustrated by working with things rather than with people. Write a clear and fully-developed essay arguing or supporting this statement. Give an example or examples which demonstrate what this statement means:

"True happiness lies in having the freedom to be the person you want to be."

Your example(s) may be taken from your personal experiences or drawn from situations you have heard or read about. You should be sure to do the following:

1. Describe your experience(s) or example(s) with specific details.
2. Explain why or how your example(s) or experience(s) show what the statement means.

✦ ✦ ✦

B. It has been suggested that anyone who truly wants to earn good grades in school can do so. However, many students go through their school years getting good grades with little effort on their part, while others struggle constantly, never managing to rise above the low end of average. Can it be true that the main ingredient in getting good grades lies in a willingness to work harder than the next person? Discuss the following statement in a clear and fully-developed essay giving an example or examples which demonstrate the truth or falsity of this statement:

"Anyone who truly wants to earn good grades in school can do so."

Your example(s) may be taken from your personal experience or drawn from situations you have heard or read about. You should be sure to do the following:

1. Describe your experience(s) or example(s) with specific details.
2. Explain why or how your example(s) or experience(s) show what the statement means.

Writing Online

Topic

Using the Computer to Communicate with Others by Writing

Objective

Students will learn how to safely and responsibly use online message boards and e-mail.

Materials

- computer with modem and telephone hook up
- access to an Internet service provider, such as America OnLine, CompuServe, or Prodigy
- reproduce copies of pages 44–46
- wall chart of E-Mail Safety Rules

Preparation

1. Reproduce pages 44–46 and prearrange an e-mail correspondent who is known to you.
2. Make a wall chart of E-Mail Safety Rules, page 46, and place it over the computers.

Procedure

1. Explain to students that writing to others by e-mail and message boards is easy and fun, but that they need to take caution about the information they give out electronically. Discuss why it is important for them to not give personal information to strangers online. The people they communicate with can soon become "pen pals" and seem like friends, but they are still strangers. Just as the students would not put their names, addresses, and phone numbers up on a billboard next to the highway, they should not give personal information online.
2. Place the transparency of Writing E-Mail on the overhead projector, and go over the steps with them. Practice writing e-mail on paper (page 44).
3. Help students go online. Do not give them your password! This allows you to control their access to the Internet. Monitor as they exchange messages with prearranged correspondents. If you wish, give them questions regarding their schoolwork to use.

Writing E-Mail

Writing to a pen pal has never been easier and, maybe, not quite as much fun as it is now because e-mail (short for *electronic mail*) is so fast and simple. Other mail seems so slow, it is often called "snail mail." All you need to use e-mail is a computer with a modem, a telephone line to hook them up to, and a service provider, which you can sign onto with software.

You can send e-mail to anyone who also has a computer with a modem, a service provider, and a telephone line if you know the e-mail screen name and address. Here is what an e-mail form looks like when it comes up on your computer monitor. (There may be some variation in this appearance, depending on the service provider, but all will contain these basic elements.)

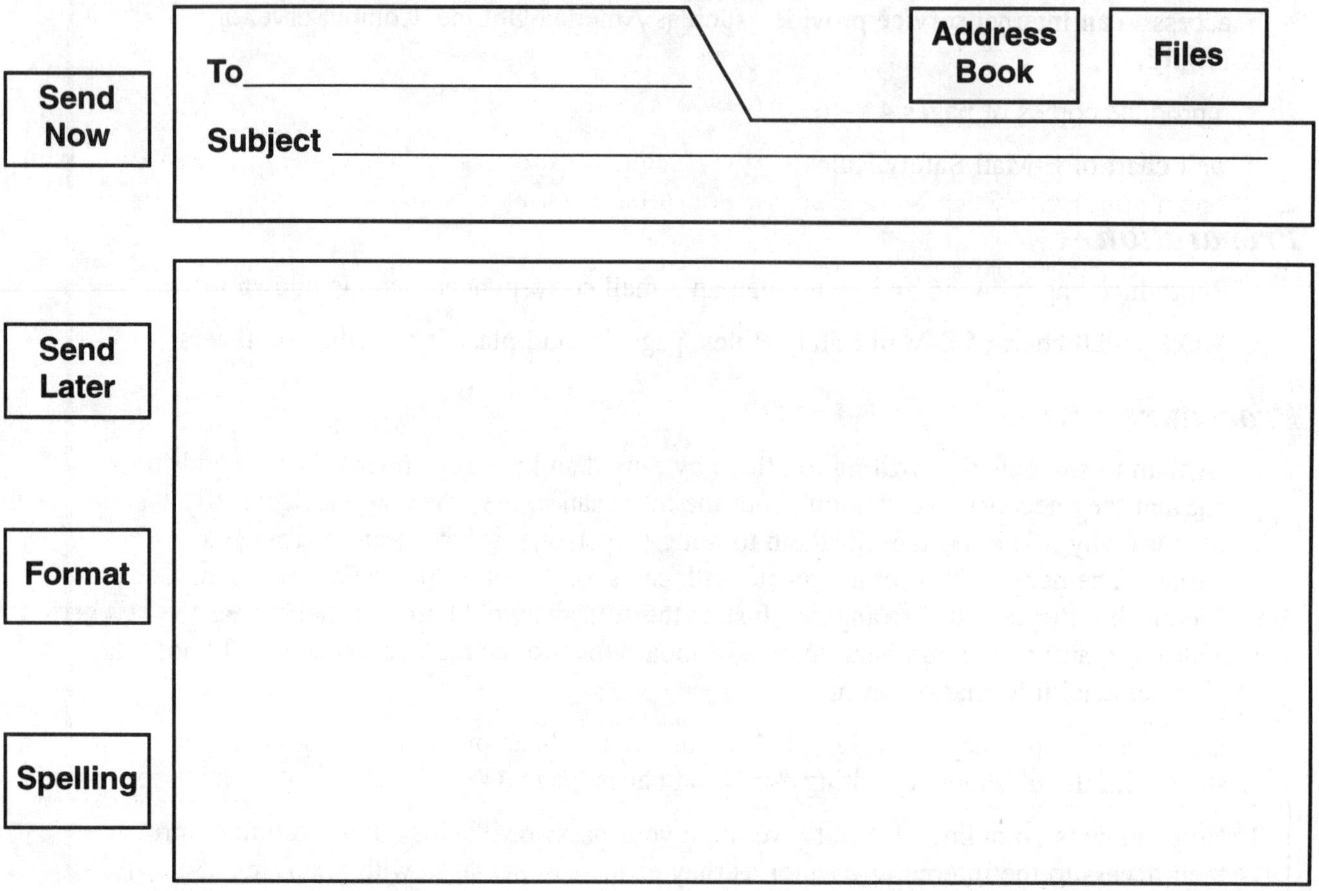

To write e-mail, do this:

1. Type in the screen name and address of the person to whom you wish to write.
2. Type in the subject of your letter.
3. Type your message. Revise and rewrite until it reads the way you want it to read.
4. When your message is finished, click on Send Now.

You can even store the e-mail screen names and addresses of all the people you plan to write in the "address book" at the top of your e-mail form. Good writing!

Using Message Boards

Discovering a new message board frequented by people who share interests with you can be as exciting as getting a new bicycle for your birthday because it opens up a whole new world of communicating with others.

There are message boards for almost every interest. One popular board is AOL's *Book Nook.* To get there, follow these steps:

1. Scroll down under "Go" to "Keyword" and type in *Book Nook.*
2. Click on the icon for Book Nook Message Boards.
3. Click on "open" for messaging 1.
4. You will see a list of categories. Highlight "Children's" and click on "Find since." Click again on "Find since." Try 1 day, which will get you the latest entries. If you have time, or if there are no new entries, work back to 2 days or 3 days, etc. A list of entries will come on the monitor with one highlighted. Click on it. There is your first message to read.

To add a message of your own, follow these steps:

1. Click on "Add message."
2. Type in your subject in the subject bar.
3. Type what you want to say in the box marked "Enter text."
4. When you have finished writing your message, click on "Post," and away it goes!

Be sure the message says what you want it to say before you click, because once it's gone, it's gone for good. The next time you see it, it will be up there on the message board for all the world to see!

It's as simple as that. And remember to use your e-mail safety rules!

> Each Internet service provider has its own message boards and means of access. Because America Online is one of the largest services and has many different boards, the instructions in this simulation are based on the typical AOL message board access. Other services will employ similar measures. You can use these boards to search for help with homework assignments, such as information about books or authors. Some services even help with homework.

E-Mail Safety Rules

(Post this reminder near your computer.)

- ❑ **Do not give your online password to anyone!**
- ❑ **When sending e-mail to strangers, do not give them your real name!**
- ❑ **When sending e-mail to strangers, do not give them your address!**
- ❑ **When sending e-mail to strangers, do not give them your telephone number!**
- ❑ **Do not send credit card numbers to anyone over the Internet!**

Most people using the Internet are honest and good, just as you are. You can have a lot of fun writing to people you don't know. You can learn a lot from them.

But you need to always keep in mind that *all you know about the stranger to whom you are writing is what that person tells you.*

It's very easy to forget to be cautious in the excitement of writing to someone who writes back to you and with whom you build an e-mail relationship. You begin to feel like friends. It's almost like writing in a diary, but it is not writing in a dairy. It is writing to someone you don't really know!

You can't see the person. You don't really know what kind of person you are writing to and who is writing to you.

Stay safe!

Follow e-mail safety rules!

Producing a Television News Magazine

Topic

Writing the Features for a Television News Magazine

Objective

Students will gather news about their school as reporters, write news feature items to be "reported" on television, edit copy, and act, produce, and direct a school news magazine for closed-circuit television or video.

Materials and Equipment

- blank paper for writing and computer paper
- pencils, pens
- video camera and/or closed-circuit television setup
- computer with word processor or typewriter (Copy can be written by hand if these are not available, but they will make possible more professional-looking copy.)
- overhead transparencies pages 51, 53, 54, and 56
- copies of pages 52, 55, 57, and 59
- sign-up sheet for Television News Magazine Staff, page 58
- overhead projector with marker
- wall chart of Television Terms, page 53

Preparation

1. Make overhead transparencies of pages 51, 53, 54, and 56.
2. Reproduce copies of pages 52, 55, 57, and 59.
3. Make a sign-up sheet for Television News Magazine Staff, page 58.
4. Make wall chart of Television News Terms, page 53.
5. Prepare a list of possible sources for student stories. Possibilities will vary from school to school.

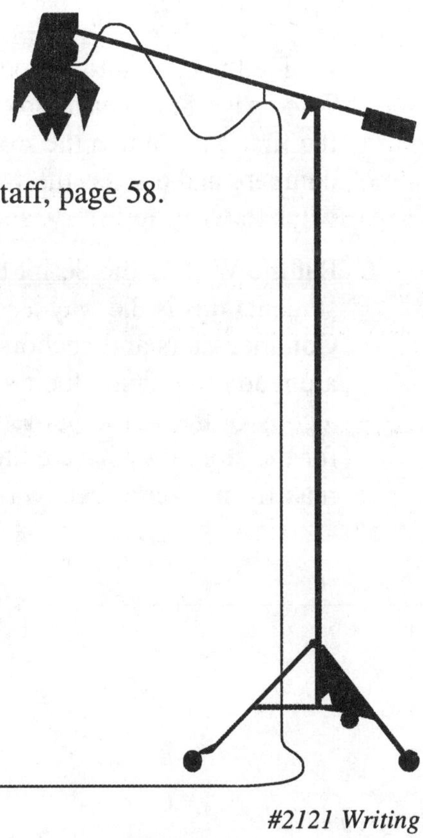

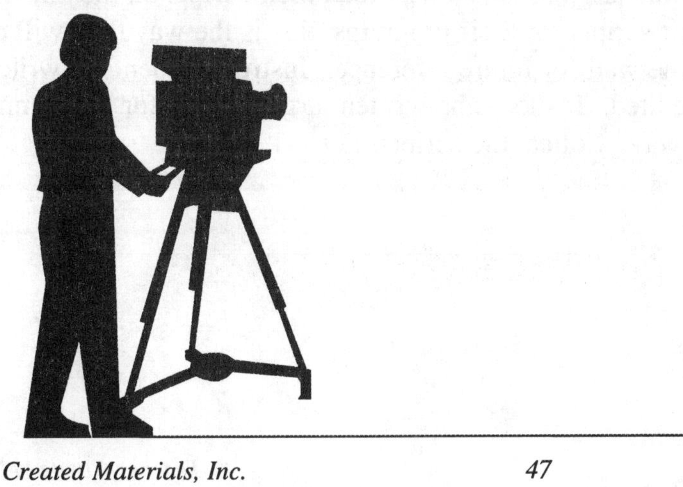

Producing a Television News Magazine *(cont.)*

Procedure

1. Inform the class that they are going to be writing and producing a television news magazine program using the same techniques that television stations use. Explain that writing a television magazine requires a lot of teamwork. Everyone must cooperate. Clear writing and strict attention to time also are necessary for the program to work.
2. The hours before a news magazine program goes on the air are very busy. New features coming in may replace others not as timeworthy. Reporters return from location sites where they have been filming their stories. They write them. In the meantime, editors and producers rewrite the stories to fit time limits. Then the stories are printed onto scripts which the commentators read on the air. Directors divide the pages of script and the video packages into set amounts of air time. The stories and the commercials are put onto schedules called rundowns.
3. Put the transparency Television Terms (page 53) on the overhead projector, and go down the list one by one. Discuss the terms and the questions about them. Tell them the wall chart showing the terms will stay on the wall so they can refer to it.
4. Put the transparency Editing Practice One (page 51) on the overhead projector. Tell the students that everything which goes on the air must be carefully edited so it will fit into the time allotted for it. Read through the original story with the students. The story must be edited to make it easier to read. Discuss the ways the story can be edited: to make it shorter, to make it clearer, to make it easier to read aloud. Tell the students they are going to edit this story together, and then do another in groups. Work on the story with students until it is short and clear. Have students rewrite the corrected stories and turn them in to you.
5. Divide the class into cooperative learning groups. Distribute copies of Editing Practice Two (page 52) to each group and instruct the students to edit this story just as they did the first one. When the stories have been edited, have students return as a class and compare and discuss the ways in which they have edited. Explain that there are many ways to write any story, and the purpose of the editing is to develop the clearest script.
6. Put the Writing the Script transparency (page 54) on the overhead projector. Tell students this is the way a script is written for a commentator to read a feature easily. Commentators and anchors are journalists who read their scripts on the air. When they are ready to prepare their scripts for their programs, this is the way they will do it. Post a copy of the script on the wall for future reference. Instruct students to write a script for the story they have edited. It should be written large enough for the commentator to read from several feet away. Collect the scripts.

Producing a Television News Magazine *(cont.)*

Procedure (cont.)

7. Tell the students that when a program is going to be aired, short commercials called teases are aired to get viewers interested in watching a feature which is going to be shown. Distribute Writing Teases (page 55). Read the instructions on the page concerning teases, and then have them write teases for the stories they have just edited.
8. Put the transparency Eyewitness Director Rundown (page 56) on the overhead projector. Tell the students this is part of a real director rundown from a real station. Discuss the parts of the rundown. There are several cameras in a television studio, and each has a number. Video and camera notations refer to the numbers of particular cameras used at a given time. Graphic refers to when pretaped videos will be used. Length refers to how long each segment will be and is noted in minutes and fractions of seconds. Emphasize how crucial timing is to producing the program; it is down to the second. Assure the students they won't have to be quite as exact, but that in their groups, they are to schedule a news magazine program as they think one might be, and to try to be as close in their timing as possible. They will use this same process in the news program which the class will be making.
9. Now it is time to begin the class' own news magazine program! They will be doing four features—one each on news, sports news, entertainment news, and important people. Divide the class into four groups according to student interest in these categories. There will be one in-depth story produced in each category. They are to signup on the sign-up sheet for the sections they will be working in. Assign producing and directing duties to individual students, and record each student's responsibility on Television News Magazine Staff (page 58).

    Commentators: For these positions, assign four students who enjoy being in the limelight but can share it with another, have a sense of the dramatic, and are good at reading orally.

    Director and Producer: Assign two students who are organized and can follow a schedule and get other students to work together well.

    Editors: There are an undetermined number of editors. If word processors or typewriters are available, editors should be able to type, or certain members of the class can be designated as typists. Since the purpose of the simulation is to write, however, typists should be allowed to write their own stories, as well as type.

    Reporters: There are an undetermined number of reporters. Some should specialize in areas such as sports, entertainment, news, and important people.

Producing a Television News Magazine *(cont.)*

Procedure (cont.)

10. On the board, list a number of suggestions you have for stories they can look for around campus. Brainstorm with them for other possibilities for stories. Suggest that they talk to the principal, secretaries, other teachers, and students of other classes for additional ideas before letting them begin. Provide help and suggestions as needed as students develop and prepare their stories. Take as many days as the students need to gather and write their stories and to schedule them on a rundown. Each class will vary.

11. When stories have been reported, edited, written into scripts, and scheduled on director rundowns, videotape the program. Assign one or more students to be videographers. Produce your news program for either closed-circuit television or tape it to be shown to the class. Share it with other classes, as well.

12. After viewing your program, discuss with the class their opinions of their success.
    - Did they write clearly?
    - Did they meet their time schedules?
    - What would they do to improve their performance, if they had it to do over again?
    - What advice would they give other classes wanting to produce a news program?

13. Present each student with a Television News Magazine Award (page 59).

Follow-Up

The students should be encouraged to watch one or more television news magazine programs to determine how closely their program followed the format of a "real" one. It would be useful to watch two or more to compare and contrast the style and content of each and to discuss the question, "Does this program seem to report the news in an unbiased fashion, or does it sometimes seem to reflect personal prejudices?"

Editing Practice One

Scripts read by the news commentators are written on the right side of a page, and everything is written in large capital letters. The first step in writing a script is editing news coming in from reporters. On another paper, practice editing the following stories which have come in from a reporter. A news feature should be based on fact, but the commentators often show their biases in the manner in which they word their features. What is this feature trying to say, and how could it be said better?

One of the many community groups in our fair city is trying to raise money to build a new sports field at the Dribble Middle School.

"Our children deserve the best," declared Mayor Marchall Hammer in his State-of-the-City speech last night. "Our children have been playing football in the mud and falling on rocks in the field. It's time to put a stop to such things happening to our children!"

"It's hard to play ball on that old field without getting your foot stuck in a gopher hole!" said Marietta Appleby as she held her four-month-old baby in her arms. "My boy got his hand stuck in a hole and got bit! This has got to stop!"

The old field was graded when the school was built way back in 1959, and it shows. Back then, nobody thought anything about a kid getting his arm or leg broken, but we know better now! The mayor says this is going to be one of his goals for the coming year.

Several service clubs in the town have already indicated their willingness to go and drum up money to help the kids.

"Kids are our main concern," said Arthur Muller, president of the Dribble Men's Fellowship Society.

After the mayor's speech, the citizens attending the meeting roundly applauded his words. You could tell by the smiles on people's faces that the mayor had hit a responsive chord among the citizens of Dribble.

Editing Practice Two

Rewrite this script so it reads well aloud.

Some people have decided they've had enough of cafeteria food. They complain it's full of fat food like cheese, pizza, and hamburgers. They complain also that it's not healthy to eat all those fat things all the time. What if someone had a heart attack right in the middle of school?

Mrs. Evangeline Heatherfield, the head cook in the cafeteria, said that she'd like to serve more healthful foods like yogurt, salad, and tofu, but that the kids won't eat it.

"They just don't know what's good for them!" she said when we interviewed her this week. "I tried to serve healthful foods once a few years ago, and the kids just wouldn't buy it!"

Now a new group has organized on campus called the Healthy Cafeteria Coalition. "Our goal is to get students healthy again," said Michael Morrison, the club's president. He said that five kids have joined the club already and they're making great strides toward having a powerful advocate for healthful food on campus.

Just what is it they want to accomplish? For one thing, they want to throw out all the ground beef in the freezers and replace it with yogurt and tofu. Then they want to eliminate all the stuff they make pizza, french fries, and corn dogs from. Finally, they want everyone to stop calling catsup a vegetable.

"Catsup is not a vegetable!" Morrison said. "It's only made from tomatoes, which are fruits, but its mostly water and sugar. Catsup is a bane in the diets of today's health conscious young people! Catsup must go!"

We took a survey of all the students. They don't think the coalition will grow very much.

Television Terms

VO	voice-over—commentator reading as video is shown
VO/SOT	voice-over/sound on tape—reader leading into taped sound bite
Package	self-contained audio-video on specific topic
Producer	one in charge of program and timing
Director	one who gets the show on the air and keeps it going on time
Editor	one who rewrites news to fit into time frame and anchor reading rate
Reporter	one who reports news on camera (Electronic News Gatherer)
Teases	20-, 30-, or 60-second previews of the coming news
Videographer	one who records news on videotape, televises show
Audio	portion of show which is heard
Visual	portion of show which is seen
Script	written portion of show, showing audio, visual, and breaks
Commentator	one who "reads" the news in front of the camera
Reading Rate	number of words a commentator or reporter reads per minute
Director Rundown	second-by-second schedule of every item on show

Writing the Script

Teleprompters holding scripts above the cameras enable commentators to read the news. Commentators must be able to read the scripts while appearing to say their lines without prompting. A real script has only two to four words to each line, so commentators can read without their eyes appearing to move from side to side. It also enables commentators to read the lines without having to look up and down from a handheld script. A page of script would look like this.

H06 Around the World

{—SplitR—}

{—aBradley—}

A TRIP AROUND THE
WORLD IS SOMETHING
MANY OF US WOULD
LOVE TO DO AT SOME
POINT IN OUR LIVES.

{—aBradley—}

WELL, ONE AMERICAN
SAYS NOW IS THE RIGHT
TIME . . . BUT HE'S NOT
TRAVELING IN THE
USUAL WAY . . . BY
AIRPLANE . . . HE'S
DOING IT USING
NOTHING BUT HOT AIR.

JOHN MILLS REPORTS.

{Cue: Take Pkg}

Write a script for a commentator to read on television from one of the stories you have edited. Write in primary-sized print with no more than two to four words to a line.

Writing Teases

Short blurbs of 15, 30, or 60 seconds are played during the hours before a television news program or a news magazine. These are called *teases*. Their purpose is to alert the viewer to certain features coming up on an upcoming program and to convince the viewer he will want to see them.

A typical tease might show the anchor or commentator who will be reading the story on the air saying,

> "What does this man (showing a picture of a man) know about the bank robbery which took place last week? He claims he knows nothing, but is that really true? The answer tonight at six o'clock on Thirty Minutes Live!"

On the lines below, write teases for each of the stories you have just edited. Include the following elements:

- a tantalizing indication of the exciting or unusual story to be shown
- the name of the program on which it will be shown
- the time the program begins

Eyewitness Director Rundown

Date: Tuesday, January 14, 1997 Time: 4:58:00 PM Out Time: 5:30:00

Page	Story/Slug	Type	Video	Camera	Graphic	OnCam	Length
A01	News ID	SOT	VTR 4	——		——	00:05
A02	At 5 #1 (McVeigh)	VO	7	DISS		aBrant	00:13
A03	At 5 #2 (Hernandez)	VO	9	WIPE		aRand	00:13
A04	At 5 # 3 (Arizona)	VO	10	WIPE		aBrant	00:13
A05	5 PM OPEN	SOT	VTR 5	5 wide		——	00:15
A06	McVeigh Trial-I	Package	11	1ts		SplitR;aBra	00:23
A07	McVeigh Trial-G	—Guts—	——	——		——	01:45
A08	Toss to Marilyn	News Room	——	1ts BOX		SplitR;aBra	00:20
A09	Hernandez Trial	VO/SOT	9–10	M nws rm/1ts		GossM	01:14
A10	Toss to Les	Live Set	——	1 ts 23s		SplitR;Ra	00:28
A11	Turturici Day 2	VO/SOT	11	L3c/23s		LBolina	01:34
A12	Rogelio Trial	VO	9	K1c		aRand	00:28
A13	Toss to Heidi	Live Bureau	——	2ts BOX		SplitR;aBra	00:13
A14	TCI: Adult Channel	VO/SOT	10	FS6/2ts		Landes	01:00
A15	Bump #1 (Crops)	VO	11	2ts		aBrant	00:15
A16	Bump #2 (Arizona)	VO	9	WIPE		aRand	00:07
B00	—BREAK—						02:00
B01	Stinger	SOT	9	——		——	00:05
B02	Missing Boat	VO	10	E2c TAG		aBrant	00:51
B03	Arizona Roads	VO	11	K3c		aRand	00:20
B04	Jet Off Runway	VO	9	WIPE		aRans	00:20
B05	Cold Wx: Crops	VO	10	E2c TAG		aBrant	00:35
B06	Cold Weather: Cats	VO/SOT	11	K3c		aBrant	01:02
B07	Bump #3 (Pet Week)	Live Set	CAM 4	1ts		SplitR;aBra	00:16
C00	—BREAK—						02:00
C01	Stinger	SOT	9	——		——	00:05
C02	Toss to Ed	Reader	——	K2c BOX		aRand	00:15
C03	Pet of the Week	Live Set	CG	3ts P4c		aBrant	02:00
C04	Toss to Weather	Reader	——	3ts Toss		Split	00:10
C05	WX/CURRENTS	VO	PBX	1ck		MrBrown	02:00
C06	WX/FORECAST	VO	PBX	1ck		——	00:00
C07	Toss to Sports	Reader	——	24s		SplitR	00:15
C08	Bump #4 (Sports)	VO	10	H3c		Finley	00:15
D00	—BREAK—						02:00
D01	Stinger	SOT	9	——		——	02:00
D02	IRSAY-COLTS	VO	10	H3fx	507	Finley	00:00
D03	KC/COACH & GM	SOT	11	H3fx	507	Finley	00:00
D04	PACKERS/SI	VO	9	H3fx	542	Finley	00:00
D05	PALMER	VO	10	H3fx	516	Finley	00:00
D06	Sports Toss Back	Reader	——	23s		——	00:10
D07	Bump #5 (Bike)	VO	11	1ts		SplitR;aBra	00:15
D08	Bump #6 (CBS Net)	SOT	9	DISS		——	00:10

Director Rundown

Every second on a television program is scheduled tightly. This ensures that all of the program itself, as well as every commercial, will appear at exactly the right time. Air time is very expensive. Advertisers pay a great deal of money to have their commercials aired, and when they sponsor a program, they want to get their money's worth. The director is the person who sees that everything goes exactly as scheduled. Use this Director Rundown form to schedule your television news magazine.

Page	Story/Slug	Type	Video	Camera	Graphic	OnCam	Length

Television News Magazine Staff

Producer ____________________

Assistant Producer ____________________

Director ____________________

Assistant Director ____________________

News Feature Producer ____________________

Sports Feature Producer ____________________

Entertainment Producer ____________________

Important People Producer ____________________

Reporters ____________________

Editors ____________________

Camera Person ____________________

Commercial Production ____________________

This

Television News Magazine Award

Is Hereby Presented

to

____

for

Excellence in News Reporting

Signed ______________________ **Date** ______________

SIMULATION #6

Writing a Novel

Topic

Writing a Class Novel

Objective

As a class and working in committees, the students will write a novel which includes setting, character development, dialogue, and plot.

Materials and Equipment

- computer with word processor or typewriter
- paper
- reproduced copies of pages 64–73
- wall chart of plot diagram, page 94
- several young adult or children's novels

Preparation

1. Obtain access to computer(s) and word processor(s) or typewriters.
2. Reproduce copies of pages 64 through 73.
3. Compile novelist's handbooks of reproduced pages 64 through 73.
4. Make a wall chart of the plot diagram (page 94).
5. Collect several good young adult or children's novels to use as examples.

Writing a Novel *(cont.)*

SIMULATION #6

Procedure

1. Tell students they are going to learn more about the novel by writing a novel as a group. Tell them that there are several types of novels, called *genres.* Give them examples of each genre. Examples might include the following:

   Romance novels having to do with love and romance, such as those by Barbara Taylor Bradford.

   Mystery novels in which detectives try to find who has committed a particular crime, such as those novels by Agatha Christie or Erle Stanley Gardner.

   Suspense novels about legal or psychological suspense such as those by John Grisham or Jonathan Kellerman.

   Western novels such as *Shane* or ones by Louis L'Amour or Zane Grey.

   Science fiction novels such as *A Wrinkle in Time* or those by Isaac Asimov or Ray Bradbury.

   Horror novels such as those in the *Goosebumps* series or those by Stephen King.

   Literary novels such as *The Red Pony, I Heard the Owl Call My Name,* or *To Kill a Mockingbird.*

   Young adult novels such as *The Outsiders, Dicey's Song,* or *The Summer of My German Soldier.*

2. Discuss the different genres of novels. Elicit from the students the names of novels they have enjoyed and categorize them according to genre. Why would you consider one to be a mystery, for example, rather than science fiction? Could a novel overlap—be considered one genre in some respects and another genre in other respects? After discussion, when you feel confident that students understand the differences among the different genres, decide as a class which genre they would like to write. Many classes will probably choose to write a mystery, although they may choose another. Take nominations from students as to which genre to write about and then have them vote.

3. Distribute novelist's handbooks to students. Tell them these handbooks contain information about many of the concerns the writer of a novel must consider. Some of the pages contain activities intended to be warmup exercises before actually beginning their novel. The activities are based on steps a real-life novelist will take in the process of writing a novel. Completing the activities will help them feel more comfortable about taking on such an extended project as writing a novel. After they have done these activities, they will be dividing into committees to work on their novel.

4. Instruct the students to turn to Showing and Telling (page 65). Read the page together. Discuss the differences between showing and telling as explained by this page. Why is showing better than telling? How will they "show" a character acting in a certain way? Have them write showing paragraphs about one or more of the sentence "telling" statements. This can be an individual or group activity.

Writing a Novel *(cont.)*

Procedure (cont.)

5. Together with the class, read Writing Dialogue and When and How to Write Dialogue (pages 66 and 67) before completing the activity at the bottom of page 66. The first page tells the purposes of dialogue in fiction and gives hints to help the student writers become more adept at writing it. The second page gives the rules for punctuating dialogue. Allowing students to refer to the pages as they work, have them write dialogue for one or more of the situations given on page 66. This can be an individual or group activity.
6. Read Creating Characters (page 68). Emphasize the importance of creating characters with whom the reader can identify; otherwise, the reader's interest will not be engaged, and he will not want to read about the characters.
7. Read Point of View (page 69). Stress that most of the novels students read are going to be in either the first or the third person. The omniscient point of view is difficult to maintain, and unless they are going to write an historical novel, there is not much point in their studying it right now. Whichever point of view they choose to use, they must remember when writing their story that the same point of view should be maintained throughout the entire story. Occasionally, professional novelists switch points of view in a story, but it can be confusing for the reader and make writing more difficult. Have them rewrite a fairy tale from a different point of view than the one they have always heard (page 69). This can be an individual or group activity.

   Note: This activity can be made more effective by reading both a traditional version of *The Three Little Pigs* and *The Real Story of the Three Little Pigs* by A. Wolf before they begin writing.
8. Read Similes and Metaphors and Outlining (pages 70 and 71) and discuss them. Stress that similes and metaphors are writing techniques that should be used sparingly to aid in description, and that they must be apt when they are used. Styles of outlining are individual, and over time they will develop ones which fit their own style of writing. Encourage them to outline in detail. Most professional writers outline plot and character clearly before ever beginning to write a novel.
9. Read and discuss Writing Action (page 72). It can't be stressed enough that the real power words of the English language are nouns and verbs. Many students come to the classroom thinking that good writing means using many adjectives and adverbs. To dispel this notion, read a random page or two from any good writer's work. Mark the passages chosen as to whether the words in them are nouns, verbs, adjectives, or adverbs. A specific verb is always better than a verb and an adverb. "Showing" the reader a person in action is always better than describing him with adjectives.

Writing a Novel *(cont.)*

Procedure (cont.)

10. Read and discuss Cause and Effect—The Truth of Fiction (page 73). Indicate the Plot Plan (page 94), and tell the students that there is nothing mysterious about plotting a story. It's simply a matter of establishing where your story begins, adding complications to the character's life, and then helping your character solve his dilemma.
11. At this point, the students may begin feeling overwhelmed by all this information. Assure them that as they work step by step through the process of writing their novel, it will gradually become more clear. They are going to work together on this project and take as long as needs to be taken. They may continue to refer to their Novelist's Handbook as they work.
12. Divide the class into four cooperative learning groups, one each to develop characters, plot, setting, and editing. (Editing members will not have work to do at this point, so they might sit in on the other groups, or their time can be spent reading a novel.) The character development committee plans a main character and two or three minor characters complete with traits, habits, clothing, style of walking, etc. The plot committee begins with a plot summary to give them their general line of action and then breaks down the summary into more detailed chapter summaries. The setting committee designs plans and maps of the area in which the novel will take place.
13. Periodically, the groups must come together to articulate with each other so as to create a natural flow of plot, character, and setting. The editing committee helps in the articulation and mechanics of the writing and works on writing style to make it consistent.
14. When the first draft of the main body is complete, the class comes together as a group to review and discuss what has been produced thus far. Does it make sense? What needs to be changed so it does make sense? They continue to rewrite and edit until they have it at a place where they want it to be. When they are at last satisfied, typists now complete the manuscript in its finished form.
15. Have each contributor to the project write a one-paragraph autobiography of himself or herself to include at the end of the project.
16. There are two possibilities for producing and distributing the finished novels. The least expensive way is to run it off via computer, collate it, and staple it. A more satisfactory way to treat the finished novel is to have it printed and bound by a professional printer, which can sometimes be done at a relatively inexpensive cost. The books can be printed in lots of one hundred, which will give each student a copy, with extras to be sold as a fund raiser to help pay printing costs. Either way, the students will have a product of which they can be truly proud.

Follow-Up

There are many aspects to writing a novel, which the students will learn while going through this process. Most important, they will learn that a writer writes with intention.

My Novelist's Handbook

Name ______________________

Name of Novel ______________________

Class ______________________ Date ______________

Showing and Telling

There is a football game after school today. You have two ways to find out what happens at the game. You can watch it, or someone can tell you about it. You would probably prefer to watch it—correct? Most people would rather see something than be told about it.

A good writer recognizes that people like to see things for themselves, so he tries to help the reader "see" what happens in his stories. What is the difference between telling and showing?

Telling, which is also called narration, is imparting information. You use it to form bridges between scenes, to recall past events without using too many words, and to sum up. You make statements about what happens.

Showing is dramatizing. Think of the story you are writing as a play taking place on a stage filled with props. To show your story, you tell it as though it were happening right in front of your eyes. Your character acts in the ways you cause him to act, and he speaks the words you give him. Compare the following examples:

> (Telling) Mrs. Ritchey is a very kind person who likes to help people.
>
> (Showing) Corabelle Ritchey strode up the flagstone path and onto the porch, a casserole dish in one hand and a bouquet of flowers in the other. "I hear your mama's feeling poorly," she said to me as she pulled open the screen door. "I just thought I'd come over and help out a spell. Now where's an apron?" She set the dish down on the kitchen table but didn't wait for an answer to her question as she headed straight for mama's bedroom. "What can I do for you, Mrs. Young? Now you just lay back on that bed and let me take care of things for a while. Don't be worryin' yourself none about the children," she said.

In which of these examples can you "see" Corabelle Ritchey? You can see her when she is acting and speaking, of course. When you just tell that she is a kind lady, the reader is apt to think, "So what?" When you enable the reader to see her and to hear her, it's a different story altogether.

Showing Practice

Turn the following "telling" statements into "showing" paragraphs.

- My Uncle Joseph is a very stingy man.
- Our paperboy is friendly but sometimes careless and thoughtless.
- My grandpa loves me a lot. He does a lot of nice things for me.
- Carol was happy at her birthday party. She got a lot of presents.
- My favorite teacher is Mr. Gentry because he's really smart and cares about the students.

Writing Dialogue

One of the most important tasks for the writer of fiction is writing dialogue. With dialogue, characters reveal themselves and each other by what they say, how they say it, and what other characters say to them. Writing dialogue sometimes causes problems for the new writer. For dialogue to be believable, it must read as though real people were actually saying the words on the page. If your dialogue sounds artificial or stilted, the reader is not going to take your characters seriously, and you will lose your reader. The following suggestions may help you write dialogue which is believable and which fits each character.

- ❑ **Listen to people speak**; then close your eyes and imagine them speaking. If you practice doing this, after awhile you will be able to give your characters words which sound like something a real person would say. Little old ladies should talk like little old ladies; a small child should talk like a small child.
- ❑ **Visualize your characters** when you have them speak. Get into the habit of moving people around inside your head and then putting words into their mouths. Put these words on paper.
- ❑ **Advance the action** of the plot with your dialogue. Don't give your characters meaningless things to say. Give them words which somehow carry the story along.
- ❑ **Vary your dialogue.** Use the word "said" when you must, but don't use it always. Sometimes use another word like *shouted*, or *screamed*, or *whispered.*
- ❑ **Break up your dialogue.** Sometimes you can break it up with action.

  "Go to bed." Mother folded back the sheets. "It's way past your bedtime."

  Sometimes you can break it up with emotion.

  "I don't want to!" Randy's small face crumpled into tears. "I'm scared!"

  But whatever your characters say, it must always help the story along.

Dialogue Practice

Write dialogue for each of the following situations:

- Two friends are discussing the death of another friend's father in an accident.
- A mother is taking her daughter out for a special lunch and a movie.
- The football coach and a player discuss strategy for the championship game.
- The school counselor and a student discuss the student's bad grades.
- Grandma and Grandpa reminisce about how they first met.

When and How to Write Dialogue

There are certain rules you need to follow when writing dialogue. They really are not difficult to learn, but they are sometimes confusing. Use these guidelines for when and how to write dialogue.

When to Write Dialogue

- to help the reader get to know the character
- to tell about what has happened before—for flashbacks
- to plant clues about what will happen later in the story
- to move along the action of the story

How to Write Dialogue

Enclose the exact words being said with quotation marks, as shown here.

Jerry said, *"I want to go home now."*

"I want to go home now," Jerry said, *"because it's getting late."*

"I want to go home." Jerry stood up. *"It's getting late."*

In these examples, you see Jerry saying basically the same thing but in different ways. The quotation marks enclose the exact words Jerry says. Nothing else.

Words like *Jerry said*, which tell who is speaking, are called *explanatory words.*

Separate the explanatory words from what is being said with a comma or commas, except when a new sentence is beginning.

In the second example above, there are commas after the word *now* and after the explanatory words *Jerry said* because *"I want to go home now because it's getting late"* is one whole sentence. In the third example above there is a period after *home* because *"Jerry"* begins a new sentence.

Capitalize the beginnings of new words and new sentences being spoken, as shown here:

Janey screamed," The car is going to crash!"

Do not capitalize the second part of a quoted sentence, as shown here:

"I wish I could go, "Tiffany said, "but I have to do my homework."

The word *but* is not capitalized because it is part of the sentence, *"I wish I could go, but I have to do my homework."*

Creating Characters

The most important part of a story is **characterization**—the portraying of characters the reader will care to read about. The reader wants to see the characters, touch them, listen to them talk, see them move around in their world, and find out what kinds of persons they are. This means the writer must see the characters clearly before writing about them in order to present living characters with good traits and bad traits, who are unique individuals but who share things in common with other people so the reader can relate to them.

There are two ways to show characters—*objectively* and *subjectively.* When you show characters objectively, you tell how they look, how they speak, how they move around, and how other people regard them. When you show characters subjectively, you help the reader feel emotionally with them by acting from inside them, by reacting to other people from inside them, and by thinking their thoughts with them. Good books have characters whom the reader can see from all their different sides. No one is all good or all bad.

Characterization Checklist

Use this checklist to guide you in creating living, breathing characters.

______ My character seems real.

______ I show my character as a whole person. I do not just list his or her physical traits nor give a feature-by-feature description of him or her.

______ I show my character in action and show the way he or she moves around his or her world.

______ I give my character a challenging situation which he or she must try to solve.

______ I show both good sides and bad sides of my character.

______ I do not praise my character so the reader will think he or she is my favorite.

______ When dealing with my character emotionally, I get deep down inside the person.

______ I give my character a name which suits that person. I do not name my villain *John Goodman*, nor do I name my heroine *Tina Tawdry*. I do not give silly names to characters I want the reader to take seriously. *Maggie Miggles* is not a good name for a heroine. Neither is *Sally Pitts*.

______ I truly like people, and this shows in my characters.

Similes and Metaphors

Similes and metaphors are literary devices which compare two unlike things to each other. A simile *likens one thing to another.* A metaphor compares one thing to another *as though they were the same.* The use of similes and metaphors helps a writer to create vivid pictures in the minds of the readers.

A simile is introduced by one of the following:

AS: **Riches fly away as the eagle flies toward heaven.**

LIKE: **An ungrateful child is like a serpent's tooth.**

SO: **As sand going through an hourglass, so are the days of our lives.**

IT REMINDS ME OF: **It reminds me of a doll I had as a young girl.**

IT MADE . . . REMEMBER: **It made Dan remember Dad's fishing pole.**

IT SEEMED AS THOUGH: **It seemed as though ants were crawling under her skin.**

IT COULD HAVE BEEN: **It could have been a bird, it was so high.**

I THOUGHT OF: **I thought of the way it was when I was a child.**

A metaphor speaks of one thing as though it actually were another without the use of a likening word.

(**Simile**) **He looked like a bear.**

(**Metaphor**) **He was a bear surrounded by little people.**

Use similes to . . .

- evoke a quick image or highlight your writing.
- shorten paragraphs of description and characterization.
- set the mood of your scenes.
- picture your characters and their settings.

Use metaphors to . . .

- create vivid images in the eye of your reader, evoke emotion, illuminate the person, object, or emotion being considered.
- bring a clear picture before the reader's eye.
- shorten paragraphs and sentences to make narration more compact.
- establish a mood or atmosphere.

Outlining

An outline can help you shape and organize your writing. It gives a pattern to follow when writing a story, whether the story is short or novel length. Some of the parts of your story which you might consider outlining include the following.

- ❑ TIME CHART: As simple as it may seem to a beginning writer, time must be measured carefully in a story. The use of a timetable can help with this. Lay out the daily schedules of your characters and keep these schedules in mind while writing so that the events in your story synchronize.
- ❑ MAPS AND HOUSE PLANS: If you are not sure of exactly where your story is laid, the reader will not be either. Draw a simple map of the area where the story takes place. Draw a floor plan of the house where the character lives with all the doors, windows, and furniture which will figure in a scene. If you choose a setting with which you are familiar, this will be easy. An imaginary scene will need more detailed planning.
- ❑ CHARACTER SKETCHES: Plan the major characteristics and traits of your principal characters and keep them in mind while you are writing. If your character is stingy, you need to show his miserly ways in his actions. Plan just enough characteristics for your characters to help them play their parts in your story.
- ❑ STORY OUTLINE: For a short story, you will need to outline by scenes. For a novel, you need to outline by chapters. Include in your outline the major events of the story and set up your conflict early because your story will need to work toward the resolution of that conflict. You might begin your outline like this.

Ransom Note

- **Chapter One:** Jason returns home from school one day to find the house empty and the screen door hanging open. He looks through the house, and his eye is caught by a piece of paper on the kitchen table. It is a ransom note which says his mother and father are being held. Jason calls the police.
- **Chapter Two:** Within minutes after Jason's call, police are all over the house, dusting for fingerprints, looking for clues, questioning Jason. The police sergeant wants to take Jason to a foster home, but Jason begs to be allowed to participate in the investigation to find his parents. At last, the police give in, and Jason is part of the investigative team.
- **Chapter Three:** Jason is teamed up with the sergeant, and together they begin a house-to-house search of the neighborhood, asking neighbors whether they have seen any suspicious-looking people around today. No one has any idea about who could have taken Jason's parents. Jason agrees to stay in the house to answer the phone, which has now been tapped.

Writing Action

There must be action in every scene of your story. Action is what draws your reader in, and action is what keeps him or her reading. There are three kinds of dramatic action—*physical action, mental action,* and *competition.*

Physical action is the kind of action you have when boxers meet in combat or when a boa constrictor swallows a mouse.

> Example: Randy reached out his long, strong arm and slapped Jonas across the face. Jonas staggered, his eyes narrowed, and he drove his head into Randy's belly. The crowd roared.

Mental action is when the action takes place inside a character's mind and emotions.

> Example: The fear started in the pit of Sarah's stomach and traveled quickly up through her chest and arms and down to her legs, turning them to jelly. "Oh, no!" she thought, "I can't go through this again! Not again!"

Competition is when there is a struggle for supremacy or for the affections of another person.

> Example: Russell Karns was out to win the race for mayor, and he used every means of slander and ridicule he and his cohorts could muster to show his opponent as corrupt, ineffective, and a total simpleton. His methods were brutal.

Your reader wants to see the action. He does not want to read a scene in which people talk about nothing in particular and do nothing. Even when people sit around the kitchen table talking or when they think silently, there still must be action to bring the scene to life. People will gesture. They will move their hands and bodies.

Use verbs to show action. Verbs are the ***action*** words, the ***power*** words, of the English language. Specific, vivid verbs are best. English contains many thousands of vivid verbs. Use a thesaurus and a dictionary to find a list of vivid verbs you can use in place of these dull, colorless ones to make your action come to life.

walk ____

said ____

fell ____

went ____

move ____

play ____

Cause and Effect—The Truth of Fiction

Imagine this scene. You sit on a bench in a large shopping mall watching people go by. You think you know what you are seeing, that the "facts" brought to you by your vision are enough to tell you what you are really seeing, but you don't. You don't know that the man leaning against the wall over there and looking like a bum has just lost his wife and is trying to make some sense of his life. You don't know that the baby in the stroller being pushed by a young mother has leukemia and isn't expected to live past the age of two. You only know what is on the surface.

Look at this diagram. What do you see? Three smooth, gray humps come out of the water. What could they be? Whales? Porpoises? Buoys?

None of the above is correct. You do not know what you are seeing, because you see only part of what is there. If you see below the water, as well as above it, you would see this. As you now know, there was more there than you thought.

The fiction writer helps the reader to see below the surface of the water, as well as above it. The fiction writer reveals what lies beneath the surface of a story and leads the reader through a chain of cause and effect to a logical conclusion. First there is a cause for an effect, then that effect becomes the cause for another effect, and that effect becomes the cause of another effect, and so it goes—on and on.

Think of a novel as being an onion. First you have the whole onion. Then you peel back a layer of the onion, then another layer, and another until you get to the onion's core. This is what the writer of a novel must do—peel back layer after layer of meaning, causes, and effects, until you have what is the central truth you want the reader to know. How do you do this in a novel?

Start with a statement . . .

Follow it with "Then because of this . . ."

"And because of this . . ."

"And because of this . . ."

"And because of this . . ."

Continue revealing causes and effects until your conclusion.

SIMULATION #7

Emergency!

Topic

Writing Historical Reports

Objective

Students will write historical reports such as are done by emergency medical technicians and police officers.

Materials and Equipment

- transparencies of pages 78, 79, 81, 82, and 84
- copies of pages 77, 80, 81, 83, and 84
- paper
- computer or typewriter
- overhead projector and marker

Preparation

1. Make transparencies of pages 78, 79, 81, 82, and 84.
2. Reproduce copies of pages 77, 80, 81, 83, and 84.
3. Arrange for computer and/or typewriter use.
4. Arrange for use of an overhead projector.
5. If possible, arrange for a visit by a police officer and/or emergency medical technician to speak to students about writing reports in their jobs. An alternative is to arrange a field trip to a police station, fire station, (most now have paramedics on staff), or ambulance company. Students think of these jobs as having glamour and do not realize that one of their most important responsibilities is writing reports.

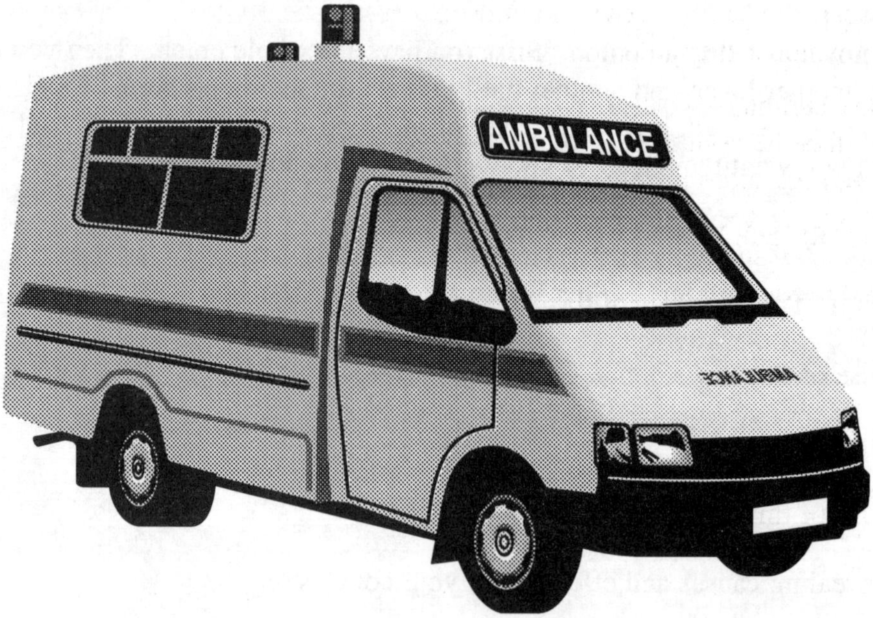

Emergency! *(cont.)*

Procedure

1. Inform students they are going to learn a new kind of writing called *historical writing*—not because it's about an event like the Civil War or the Industrial Revolution, but because it is written to record what is happening right now but will be history once it is over. Tell them historical writing seems easy. They don't have to develop characters or write proper paragraphs with topic sentences as they do in writing fiction or essays. They do have to write in detail and with accuracy, recording exactly what is happening, or has happened, in a situation. It is the kind of writing done by doctors, nurses, firefighters, paramedics, and police officers.
2. Arrange for a visit from police officers or emergency medical technicians (optional but desirable), or a field trip to the paramedics of a fire station or a police station to visit with professionals for whom writing reports is a daily necessity.
3. Distribute Historical Writing (page 77). Read and discuss the information together until you are certain the students understand the concept of historical writing. Tell the students there are different forms of historical writing used by people in various disciplines, and that they are going to learn two kinds: that done by police officers and that done by paramedics.
4. Display the first page of Crime Report (page 78) on the overhead projector. Explain this is the first page of a typical report filled out by police officers when a crime is encountered by them, probably several times per day. Indicate the various aspects of the page. Not only must an officer record all the factual information about a victim of a crime and the witnesses to it (including their addresses, phone numbers, driver's license numbers, and a brief description of those people), but he also must know the precise number of the criminal code which refers to the crime committed. When the report is completed, it must be signed by the officer and the commanding officer.
5. Display page 2 of the crime report (page 79) on the overhead projector. Indicate to the students that on this page the officer records all the vital information needed about the vehicle involved in a crime. Here the officer also records a description of the suspect. If the suspect is at the scene, the information may be obtained from him then. If the suspect is not at the scene, a description is taken from any witnesses to the crime.
6. The case summary which is written in the lower part of page 2 is as important as the factual data the police officer collects at the scene of the crime. This summary is a one-paragraph narration in chronological order of exactly what has happened. Because it is part of a legal document, it must be precise and accurate. To practice writing a chronological summary such as one a police officer must write, dictate the following fictional account of an incident which students are to record in a one-paragraph summary.

Emergency! *(cont.)*

Procedure (cont.)

Jennifer Cortez was waiting in line in a convenience store when an armed gunman ran into the store and pushed a gun in the face of the clerk. "Give me all the money in your cash register right now!" he shouted. Still watching the clerk, he turned to the four people standing in line and shouted, "Turn your faces around to the back of the store and put your hands up!" Jennifer was standing in line to pay for a soda and was startled. The gunman wore a ski mask, a black sweatshirt, jeans, and dark glasses. Jennifer began to cry because she was so scared. "Count to 10 before you turn around!" the gunman said, collecting the money; then he backed out the door and ran around the side of the building. The clerk called the police.

Have students fill out the Crime Report (page 81) and write a one-paragraph summary of the incident with the information given. In the paragraph, write only the necessary facts and write them in the exact order in which they happened. Will you need to write that Jennifer cried? No. Will you need to write that the gunman wore a mask? Yes. Discuss any problems or questions the students have.

7. Display the Prehospital Care Report (page 82). Explain that this is the kind of report a paramedic must fill out for every patient. Note that information on this form consists of medical data with a detailed description of the patient's physical condition, including injuries and data regarding the patient's allergies and medical history. "Chief complaint" would be the reason a paramedic was called. Instead of a summary such as a police officer writes, a paramedic lists events and the times when they occur. Time is given in military time—that is, in number of hours since 12:00 midnight. In military time two P.M. would be 14:00 hours. On this particular report we have the following:

   23:20 Arrived on scene—assessed pt. (patient)
   23:25 Extricated from car with spine precautions
   23:26 Vital signs taken (blood pressure, pulse rate, respiration)

8. Read the Emergency Incident (page 84) to students. They are going to write crime reports and prehospital care reports for this incident. Divide the class into cooperative learning groups. Distribute to each group a blank crime report (page 81), a blank Prehospital Care Report (page 83), and a copy of the Emergency Incident (page 84). Elicit from students that this incident is a crime because the driver of the car left the scene of the accident, which is *hit and run*—a crime. Instruct each group to assign one person as recorder for the group, and to choose this person carefully because the report must be very neat. When the activity is complete, discuss the student's results. This activity may be repeated as often as needed until students are competent report writers.

Background/Follow-Up

It is said that over 90 percent of police recruits who do not make it onto the force fail because they are unable to write clear and accurate reports. The same is true for paramedics, nurses, and doctors. Clear, accurate reports are essential for success in any of these fields.

Point of View

A writer of fiction writes with what is called a **voice**. The writer takes a stand. He gives life to characters and situations, and he wants to tell this story from the best and most dramatic position possible. The place he chooses to speak from is called **point of view**. The point of view used by the author of a novel is usually one of these shown below.

First person • Third person • Omniscient

- ❑ **A story told from the first person point of view is an "I" story.** One of the characters in the story tells it the way he saw it happen. This character may be the hero or heroine of the story. In this point of view, the personality, feelings, motivations, fears, hopes, and frustrations of that character are revealed to the reader by him.
- ❑ **A story told from the third person point of view is a "he" or "she" story.** In the third person point of view, the writer still tells the story from the viewpoint of a character, but the character is always referred to as "he" or "she." We still may be told what the character is thinking and feeling, but it will be "he thought" or "she felt."
- ❑ **A story told from the omniscient point of view goes within the minds of all the characters.** There is no suspense in this story, as there may be in other points of view, because the reader already knows what's going to happen. An historical novel often is told from the omniscient point of view because the outcome is already known.

To help understand point of view, consider the story of *The Three Little Pigs.*

- If one of the pigs or the wolf tells the story the way he saw it happen and calls himself "I," the story is written in **the first person**.
- If the story is told from the point of view of one of the pigs or the wolf, but that character is called "he," the story is written in **the third person**.
- If we can see into all of the character's minds, the story is in **the omniscient point of view**.

Tell these stories from different points of view:

1. *Cinderella* from the point of view of a stepsister.
2. *Snow White* from the point of view of one of the seven dwarfs.
3. *Little Red Riding Hood* from the point of view of the wolf.

Historical Writing

The kind of writing done by EMT's (paramedics), police officers, and medical personnel is called historical writing because it sets down in chronological order and in black and white the "history" of a case. The historical writing done by a policeman consists of case summaries detailing the facts of a crime or accident. The historical writing done by EMT's and medical personnel consists of anecdotal records (also called notes or logs) detailing medical facts observed about the patient and what was done for him.

When EMTs write a report, they don't have to create characters or develop plot and dialogue, or use the literary devices a novelist uses. What they do have to do is be detailed and accurate. Everything must be recorded on a permanent record exactly as it happened, and while paperwork isn't exciting, it is vital to their doing a competent job. The information they write must be kept permanently because any incident may at some point become the focus of a court proceeding.

The key words in historical writing are *detail* and *accuracy.* A detailed, accurate report benefits both the EMT and the patient. The patient benefits because those who take over his or her care from the EMT have a record of the patient's condition when he or she was first encountered by the EMT and what has been done since. The EMT benefits because a detailed, accurate medical record is his or her best protection if the case is ever the subject of a court proceeding. Legally, if something was done but not written down, it wasn't done at all. It goes without saying that the report must be done neatly.

Read carefully the Prehospital Care Report. This is an exact copy of a form used by an EMT. The first half of the form records the facts when the patient is first seen: the name, address, age, chief complaint (the reason an EMT has been called), medical history (any long-term medical problems like diabetes), allergies, and any medications taken regularly. This information is obtained from the patient when the person is first seen, unless he or she is unconscious. Then it must be obtained some other way. The patient's initial physical examination records any obvious injuries or conditions the EMT sees.

The second half of the form records exactly what was done for the patient by the EMT, who did it, at what time, how the patient responded to what was done, and the patient's *vital signs* (blood pressure, pulse rate in number of beats per minute, and respiratory rate in number of breaths per minutes).

The bottom of the report indicates any special conditions at the scene and safety equipment used and where the patient was transferred. The EMT and whoever took over from him both sign the report.

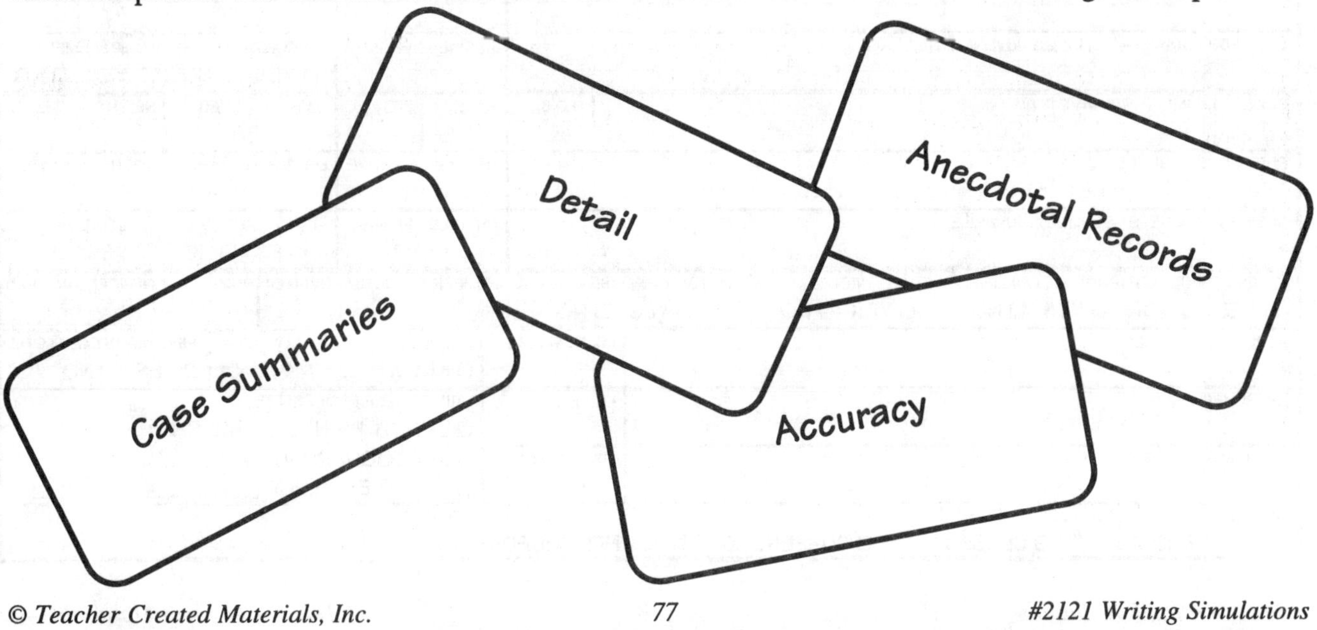

AGENCY **CA 04803**	CITY OF FAIRFIELD POLICE DEPARTMENT **CRIME REPORT**	CASE NUMBER

COPY TO	DA	PROB	D.O.J.	INV.	Y.S.B.	S.O.D.	RO	PRESS	JUV. HALL	OTHER	PAGE NUMBER

PRIMARY CRIME CODE	SECONDARY CRIME CODES	CLASS CODE	INDEXED BY

DATE & TIME OCCURRED	DATE & TIME REPORTED	LOCATION OF OCCURRENCE

VICTIMS & WITNESSES ONLY

DESIGNATOR CODES: V=VICTIM W=WITNESS

CODE	NAME—FIRM NAME IF BUSINESS	D.O.B.	RACE	SEX	HAIR	EYES	HEIGHT	WEIGHT
RESIDENCE ADDRESS			RESIDENCE PHONE	DRIVER'S LICENSE NUMBER				STATE
BUSINESS ADDRESS—SCHOOL IF JUVENILE			BUSINESS PHONE	CONTACTED ❑ YES ❑ NO		STATEMENT ❑ YES ❑ NO		
CODE	NAME—FIRM NAME IF BUSINESS	D.O.B.	RACE	SEX	HAIR	EYES	HEIGHT	WEIGHT
RESIDENCE ADDRESS			RESIDENCE PHONE	DRIVER'S LICENSE NUMBER				STATE
BUSINESS ADDRESS—SCHOOL IF JUVENILE			BUSINESS PHONE	CONTACTED ❑ YES ❑ NO		STATEMENT ❑ YES ❑ NO		
CODE	NAME—FIRM NAME IF BUSINESS	D.O.B.	RACE	SEX	HAIR	EYES	HEIGHT	WEIGHT
RESIDENCE ADDRESS			RESIDENCE PHONE	DRIVER'S LICENSE NUMBER				STATE
BUSINESS ADDRESS—SCHOOL IF JUVENILE			BUSINESS PHONE	CONTACTED ❑ YES ❑ NO		STATEMENT ❑ YES ❑ NO		
CODE	NAME—FIRM NAME IF BUSINESS	D.O.B.	RACE	SEX	HAIR	EYES	HEIGHT	WEIGHT
RESIDENCE ADDRESS			RESIDENCE PHONE	DRIVER'S LICENSE NUMBER				STATE
BUSINESS ADDRESS—SCHOOL IF JUVENILE			BUSINESS PHONE	CONTACTED ❑ YES ❑ NO		STATEMENT ❑ YES ❑ NO		
CODE	NAME—FIRM NAME IF BUSINESS	D.O.B.	RACE	SEX	HAIR	EYES	HEIGHT	WEIGHT
RESIDENCE ADDRESS			RESIDENCE PHONE	DRIVER'S LICENSE NUMBER				STATE
BUSINESS ADDRESS—SCHOOL IF JUVENILE			BUSINESS PHONE	CONTACTED ❑ YES ❑ NO		STATEMENT ❑ YES ❑ NO		
CODE	NAME—FIRM NAME IF BUSINESS	D.O.B.	RACE	SEX	HAIR	EYES	HEIGHT	WEIGHT
RESIDENCE ADDRESS			RESIDENCE PHONE	DRIVER'S LICENSE NUMBER				STATE
BUSINESS ADDRESS—SCHOOL IF JUVENILE			BUSINESS PHONE	CONTACTED ❑ YES ❑ NO		STATEMENT ❑ YES ❑ NO		

DOMESTIC VIOLENCE	PROP 115 QUALIFIED	VICTIM OF VIOLENT CRIME	VICTIM RESPONSE - 293 P.C.	NUMBER OF VICTIMS OVER 60	NUMBER OF OFFICERS INJURED
❑ YES ❑ NO	❑ YES ❑ NO	❑ YES ❑ NO	❑ YES ❑ NO		

REPORTING OFFICER	I.D. NUMBER	SUSPECT ❑ KNOWN ❑ UNKNOWN	NEIGHBORS CONTACTED ❑ YES ❑ NO
APPROVED BY	I.D. NUMBER	CRIME SCENE PROCESSED: ❑ LATENT PRINTS ❑ SKETCH ❑ PHOTOGRAPHED ❑ OTHER EVIDENCE ____________	
FOLLOW-UP ASSIGNED TO	I.D. NUMBER		
CASE STATUS: ❑ PENDING ❑ CLOSED ❑ SUSPENDED ❑ UNFOUNDED		RELATED CASES	

INVOLVED VEHICLES/BOATS

DESIGNATOR CODES: V=VICTIM S=SUSPECT

CASE #

CODE	LICENSE/REG. NUMBER	STATE	YEAR	MAKE	MODEL	BODY/HULL STYLE
	COLOR	OTHER CHARACTERISTICS			DISPOSITION OF VEHICLE	
CODE	LICENSE/REG. NUMBER	STATE	YEAR	MAKE	MODEL	BODY/HULL STYLE
	COLOR	OTHER CHARACTERISTICS			DISPOSITION OF VEHICLE	

SUSPECT DESCRIPTION

CODE	NAME—FIRM NAME IF BUSINESS	D.O.B.	RACE	SEX	HAIR	EYES	HEIGHT	WEIGHT
RESIDENCE ADDRESS			RESIDENCE PHONE		DRIVER'S LICENSE NUMBER			STATE
BUSINESS ADDRESS—SCHOOL IF JUVENILE			BUSINESS PHONE		CONTACTED ❑ YES ❑ NO		STATEMENT ❑ YES ❑ NO	
ADDITIONAL DESCRIPTION								

CODE	NAME—FIRM NAME IF BUSINESS	D.O.B.	RACE	SEX	HAIR	EYES	HEIGHT	WEIGHT
RESIDENCE ADDRESS			RESIDENCE PHONE		DRIVER'S LICENSE NUMBER			STATE
BUSINESS ADDRESS—SCHOOL IF JUVENILE			BUSINESS PHONE		CONTACTED ❑ YES ❑ NO		STATEMENT ❑ YES ❑ NO	
ADDITIONAL DESCRIPTION								

CODE	NAME—FIRM NAME IF BUSINESS	D.O.B.	RACE	SEX	HAIR	EYES	HEIGHT	WEIGHT
RESIDENCE ADDRESS			RESIDENCE PHONE		DRIVER'S LICENSE NUMBER			STATE
BUSINESS ADDRESS—SCHOOL IF JUVENILE			BUSINESS PHONE		CONTACTED ❑ YES ❑ NO		STATEMENT ❑ YES ❑ NO	
ADDITIONAL DESCRIPTION								

CASE SUMMARY

Police Reports

One type of historical writing is the writing of police reports. Writing accurate, detailed reports is one of the most important parts of being a police officer. Crime reports are similar to those of emergency medical technicians in that they deal with facts, but rather than concentrating on the medical facts of a case, a police report concentrates on events that happened, who was involved, and whether a crime has been committed.

When a police officer arrives on the scene where an incident has taken place, he notifies the emergency people if they are needed and immediately begins asking questions, taking informal notes to determine exactly what has happened, and recording it. He interviews all the people involved and all the witnesses, recording names, addresses, phone numbers, and everything relevant which is told to him. If it is determined that a crime has taken place, the officer writes a crime report.

A standard crime report is a form of two pages or more on which the officer records all the necessary statistical information. It includes information about everyone who witnessed the incident: the name and description of the suspect or suspects, if any are known; the model, make and color of any vehicle involved; and the victim's name, address, and phone number.

Along with filling out the form of a crime report, the officer must write a *summary* of the incident. A summary is a detailed narration of exactly what happened, and events must be told in the exact order in which they happened. The officer will not try to make his summary exciting or colorful because the police are concerned only with the facts which are important to the case.

A summary must be precise because it becomes a legal document. If the incident develops into a court proceeding, the crime report becomes very important. The police officer may be required to go to court as a witness, and since no police officer could be expected to remember every detail of every incident which happens, he will rely on his report as the basis for his testimony. A summary might read like this:

> Johnny Jones reported that he laid his bicycle on his front lawn to run into the house for a minute, and when he came back out, the bicycle was gone without his permission. Harley Davis, a neighbor, saw a boy of about 14 walking down the street who ran to the bicycle, got on it, and rode it away.

This summary is a straightforward account of what happened and establishes the fact that someone took a bicycle without the permission of the owner. It summarizes the events which took place in the order in which they took place. Other parts of the form will describe the stolen bicycle and will identify the persons involved so far as they are known.

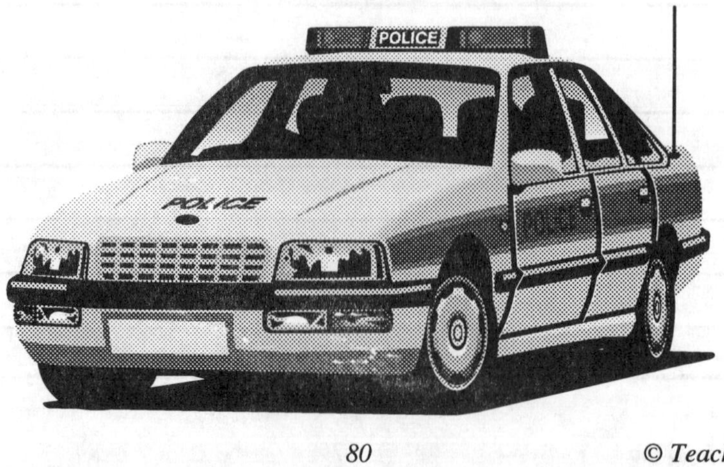

Crime Report

City of ______________________________ Date ______________

Victim ______________________________ Date of Birth ___________

Witness #1

Name ______________________________ Age ______________

Address ____

Witness #2

Name ______________________________ Age ______________

Address ____

Involved Vehicle Make ____________________ License # ____________

Color ______________________________

Suspect Description:

Name ______________________________

Approximate Age _______ Height ________ Weight _______

Color Hair ______________ Color eyes ____________

Distinguishing Characteristics ______________________________

____

Case Summary

____

____

____

____

____

____

____

Reporting Officer ________________ Approved by ________________

Prehospital Care Report

Call Date	Provider Number	Unit Number	Incident Number	Inter-Facility Transfer Number	Call disposition
2-18-97	683	021	86652398989	0003987	64

Response Code	Transport	Time Of Call	Time Enroute	Time Arrived On Scene	Time Left Scene/ Call Cancelled	Time Arrived At Destination	Base Hospital Contact	Time Of Base Hospital Contact
❑ 1 ❑ 2 ☒ 3	❑ 1 ❑ 2 ❑ 3	23:13	:06	23:19	23:42	23:56	☒ Made ❑ Attempted ❑ Not attempted	23:25

Patient Name (Last, First, MI)	Patient Address	Incident Location
Doe, Jane J.	286 Mrytle St. Anytown, USA 00000	1500 block Cedar & Vine

Patient Age	Patient DOB	Patient Gender	EST. Patient Weight	County	Map Zone	Number Of Patients At Scene
56 ❑ Months ☒ Years	6-22-41	❑ Male ☒ Female	88 kg	03	621555	01

Chief Complaint right leg pain, chest pain, shortness of breath

Allergies penicillin, iodine, tape

Medical History Diabetes > 5 yrs., Hypertension > 5 yrs.

Medications glucophage, glucotrol, Capoten, Lopressor

Initial Physical Examination

	Unremarkable	
Head	❑	small laceration right side forehead with large hematoma
Neck	☒	
Chest	❑	bruising to center of chest
Abdomen	❑	large distended, nontender
Back	☒	
Pelvis	☒	
Limbs	❑	both legs multiple lacerations, right lower leg swelling
Neuro	❑	lethargic, confused
Skin Signs	❑	pale, cool, diaphoretic

GCS

Eye	Verbal	Motor
4 spont	5 oriented	6 obeys
3 voice	4 confused	5 localizes
2 pain	3 inapprop	4 withdrwl
1 none	2 incompr	3 flexion
	1 none	2 extension
		1 none

Time	E	V	M	Total
23 : 19	4	4	6	14
23 : 28	3	4	6	13
23 : 55	3	4	5	12

Mechanism Of Injury 03

Types Of Illness/Injury 010, 007, 015

Field Clinical Impression MVA—head on collision with larger vehicle. Possible head injury, fractured tib/fib R

Care Giver	Time	Procedure/Medication Description		Response/Comments	Blood Pressure	Pulse Rate	Resp Rate
A+B	23:20		Arrived on scene-assessed Pt.		/	110	24
A+B	23:25	002	Extricated from car—Cspine precautions)		/		
B	23:26	010	Vital signs	LOCX3, breath sounds clear bilat.	158/ 90	112	20
A+B	23:27		Pt in back of ambulance on backboard		/		
A	23:29	012	IV NS #20g cath R	LOCX2	/		
A+B	23:35	344	R Lwr leg spinted, c/o chest pain BS R base c crackles		170/ 95	121	28
A	23:36	312	Base contact, further instruction 02 sats 95%		/		
B	23:37		Enroute to hospital		/		
A	23:45	262	Pt c/o severe chest pain—morphine sulfate 5 mglV		175/110	122	24
A	23:47	015	Fluid bolus 250 Ml		/		
A+B	23:56		Arrived base hospital		/		
A	24:00		Report given to nurse		148/ 92	110	20
	:				/		
	:				/		
	:				/		
	:				/		
	:				/		

Special Scene Conditions		Safety Equipment Used	MVA Conditions	Destination Decision Reason	
❑ ALS w/o base hosp. contact	❑ MCI	☒ Lap restraint	☒ Bent steering wheel	❑ Nearest receiving facility	Receiving Hospital 0341
☒ Complicated extrication	❑ Mult. EMS providers	❑ Lap/shoulder restraint	❑ Death in same vehicle	❑ Base order	Base Hospital 0341
❑ DNR	❑ Poss. provider exposure	❑ Child safety seat	❑ Ejection	❑ Diversion	Base MD Kerr
❑ Drug use susp.	❑ Unsafe scene	❑ Airbag	❑ Passenger compartment intrusion	❑ Physical requested	MICN Barton
❑ ETOH use susp.	❑ Other ________	❑ Helmet	❑ Rollover	☒ Pt/Family requested	
☒ Hazardous material		❑ Protective clothing		❑ Triage to trauma center	
				❑ Triage to other specialty center	
				❑ Other	

Care Transferred To
Agency Anywhere Hospital | Time 24:00
Name

	Cert. Number	Name (print)	Signature
A)	5439	James P. Medic	
B)	1718	Nancy Johnson	
C)			

Prehospital Care Report

Date__________ Unit Number________________ Incident Number____________________________

Patient Name________________________ Patient Address ______________________________________

Patient Age______________ Patient DOB_________ Patient Gender_____________ Patient Weight ________

Chief Complaint__________________________________ Allergies ______________________________

____

Medical History____ Medications_________________________

____

____

Initial Physical Examination	Special Scene Conditions
Head	
Neck	
Chest	
Abdomen	Safety Equipment Used
Back	
Pelvis	
Limbs	
Neuro	Motor Vehicle Conditions
Skin Signs	

Care Giver	Time	Procedure/Medication Description	Response/Comments	Blood Pressure	Pulse Rate	Resp. Rate

Care Transferred to	Name	Signature
Agency	Time	
Name		

Emergency Incident

Using the information in this incident as described here, write prehospital care and police reports as directed.

July 15, 1997, 2:15 P.M.

Kelly Pearson, age 13, and Janet Jensen, age 14, were waiting for the bus at the corner of Grant and Main Streets when they noticed a 1990 Chevrolet driving erratically down Grant Street. Just as the car reached the corner, a boy named Jessie Jameson, age 11, came riding down Main Street on a bicycle. He and the car collided. There was a loud crash from the bike hitting the car, and the boy was thrown approximately 10 feet from where the car hit him. The car slowed down momentarily but did not stop.

Kelly got a partial license number—California 2 BTW . . . . The driver was a white male in his twenties with brown hair. The boy thrown from the bicycle was moaning, and there was a lot of blood.

Susan Windham, the driver of another car, who had seen the incident from half a block away, stopped and called 911 from her cell phone and then got out to help. The two girls were very scared and began to cry. Ms. Windham quickly got a coat and put it over the injured boy who was shivering and crying in pain.

Windham could tell his arm was broken because of the strange angle at which it lay, and his leg was twisted underneath him and might have also been broken. His face had many cuts and bruises, and his eye was quickly swelling shut where he had landed on it. Ms. Windham continued to talk to him quietly, telling him that she had called an ambulance and he would have help soon.

Just then, a police car arrived. Two officers got out, and one ran over to where the boy was lying to see whether he could help with first aid. The other officer spoke into his car radio and then got out a pad and began asking questions of the two girls and the woman while the first officer stayed with the boy. The females answered the officer's questions and one at a time told the officer what they had witnessed.

The ambulance arrived, and two paramedics got out and ran to where the boy was lying. One then ran back, got a gurney, some splints, and a blanket and brought them to where the boy lay. Two more police cars arrived to help. The first paramedic began checking the boy all over, asking whether this hurt and that. The EMT got the boy's name and phone number, and a police officer went to the car radio to call the parents. The EMT's could see the arm was going to need a doctor's help, also the leg. They immobilized the arm and leg and gently placed the boy on the gurney. One took his blood pressure. It was 132/80. His eyes were glassy with pain. His face was bleeding. His temperature was 99.1 degrees Fahrenheit and he was breathing about 25 breaths per minute.

His mother arrived just as the EMT's were putting the gurney into the ambulance. The officer questioned her a minute. "I have to go with my son," she said, and got into the ambulance with him, leaving her car parked at the side of the street. The officer told the girls and Ms. Windham that the police would be contacting them later. They removed the broken bicycle from the street and directed traffic around the scene as it was happening.

Entering the Park Service

SIMULATION #8

Topic

Writing an Autobiography as Part of a Job Application

Objective

Students will write a 250-word autobiography as part of an application for a summer job with the park service.

Materials and Equipment

- computer and/or typewriter
- paper
- reproduced copies of pages 87 and 88
- transparency of pages 87 and 88
- overhead projector and marker

Preparation

1. Make transparency of pages 87 and 88.
2. Reproduce copies of pages 87 and 88.
3. Arrange for use of a computer and/or typewriter.
4. Arrange for use of an overhead projector.

Procedure

1. Tell students they are going to practice applying for a summer job with the park service and that many applications require some sort of autobiography for the application to be complete. The application may not say "Write an autobiography" as this application does. It may have another question such as, "On the back of this paper, tell in one page or less why you are a good candidate for this position," or it may say, "With this application, include a summary of your prior experience which qualifies you for this position." There are many ways of wording a request for an autobiography. The purpose of this portion of an application is let the employer judge your writing skill and learn things about you that pertain to the job. This is an excellent example of one of the many ways in which you must always write for your reader. In this case, your reader is the person from whom you are seeking a summer job.

Entering the Park Service *(cont.)*

SIMULATION #8

Procedure (cont.)

2. Display the transparency of the Park Service Application on the overhead projector. Create an imaginary person and, with the students, complete the application as it would be completed by that person. The items on the application are generally straightforward and do not need explanation. Nevertheless, stress that it is necessary to type or print an application neatly. All items should be answered fully. If students need more room to list experience or special training, it can be done on a separate page. Tell students that an application which is not neat or complete will probably be "filed" in the waste basket because employers want to hire people who care enough to treat their applications appropriately.
3. Display the Autobiography Outline (page 88) on the overhead. Explain that an autobiography should be carefully thought out and planned before its submission to a prospective employer. This employer wants to learn those things about an applicant which are relevant to a job, so this is what an applicant should stress. He does not want an applicant to merely repeat what he has already included in the application form, such as vital statistics. If an autobiography is well-planned and neatly written, it will have a much better chance of catching the eye of the employer. Using the fictional person on the application, complete the outline with students.
4. When students are clear about the goals of their applications and autobiographies, distribute copies of pages 87 and 88 for them to complete about themselves. Caution them to include only factual information because they would not want a prospective employer to learn that they had submitted false information. That would lose them any chance of getting the job. In their autobiographies they can include any information about their hobbies or interests which are relevant to the job. When students have completed their applications and autobiographies, interview them one at a time and tell them how successful the application (including the autobiography) is.

Background/Follow-Up

As we go further into the "Information Age," being able to write well and to communicate well with others becomes more crucial to one's success. A job application is the first encounter a prospective employer has with an applicant. How well the applicant meets the employer's standards within the application format will determine whether the applicant goes all the way to acceptance as an employee.

Park Service Application

Complete the following completely and accurately. Do not leave any spaces blank.

Name ______________________________ Date ______________

Address ____

Telephone ____________________________ Fax ____________

Educational Background

Total Years Education ______________ Grade-Point Average ____________

Last School Attended ______________________ Dates ____________

Educational Major and Minor ______________________________

Plans for Future Education ______________________________

Work Experience

Date ____________ to ____________ Job Title ______________

Employer ____

Employer Address ______________________________________

Date ____________ to ____________ Job Title ______________

Employer ____

Employer Address ______________________________________

Special Training

Date ____________ to ____________ Job Title ______________

School/Trainer Name ____________________________________

References ____

____

On the back of this page or on a separate sheet of paper, write an autobiography in 250 words or less, telling why you would be good at the position for which you are applying. If you need extra space for any response, use a separate sheet.

Autobiography Outline

An autobiography of 250 words will occupy about one double-spaced typewritten page. In this page you want to tell your prospective employer all those good things about yourself which will make him want to hire you, those things that you have not told him on the application form. You are applying for a summer job with the park service with the following job description:

> **Job Description:** Sell souvenirs in gift shop. Help visitors to the park and make change. Provide assistance when needed to elderly visitors. Clean restrooms. Rake leaves and do occasional outdoor work. Applicant must work well with others and be prompt and courteous at all times. Must show an interest in protecting the environment.

In your autobiography, you want to emphasize all the interests and experiences you have had which fit in with the above description. The following outline is an example:

I. **Interests:** Discuss those interests which are related to parts of the job description at which you feel you will be very good.

- A. You make spending money in the fall by raking leaves.
- B. You often take your grandfather, who is in a wheelchair, for walks.
- C. For the past two years you have gone once each month with your church youth group to entertain old people in the senior citizen's home.
- D. Your favorite class in school was the ecology class you took last fall, and you are a member of the school Sierra Club.
- E. Your hobby is collecting leaves and pressing them.

II. **Special Abilities:** Discuss those special abilities you have which are related to parts of the job description.

- A. You have taken business math in school and know how to use a cash register.
- B. You are responsible for keeping the lawn mowed at home and are able to use a riding lawn mower.
- C. You are vice chairman of the Junior Achievers at school and work well with others in that capacity.

Do you get the idea? Use your outline as an organizational tool to structure your autobiography. Then, without bragging, write confidently about your abilities.

Writing a Letter of Complaint

SIMULATION #9

Topic

Writing a Letter to a Manufacturer Regarding a Faulty Product

Objective

Students will write a letter to a manufacturer regarding a pair of sneakers, the soles of which cracked and pulled apart after only one month's use.

Materials and Equipment

- computer with word processor or typewriter
- paper
- transparency of page 92
- reproduced copies of pages 91–93
- overhead projector and marker

Preparation

1. Make transparency of page 92.
2. Reproduce copies of pages 91–93.
3. Arrange for use of a computer and/or typewriter.
4. Arrange for use of an overhead projector.

SIMULATION #9

Writing a Letter of Complaint *(cont.)*

Procedure

1. Explain to the students that at times it is necessary to write a letter to a manufacturer. Sometimes a product does not live up to the expectations of the consumer in some way. The product may have been faulty when it was manufactured, or it may have become damaged between the time it left the manufacturer and reached the consumer. Usually, manufacturers are willing to settle disputes with the consumer. The good will of the consumer is important to a manufacturer, and if a consumer writes a well-thought-out letter, the faulty product will probably be replaced or repaired.
2. Distribute copies of Planning Your Letter (page 91) and read it with the class. Stress the Do's and Don'ts of writing a letter to a manufacturer. Elicit from students any experience any of them have had with faulty sneakers or other products. Tell them that after they finish this simulation they will be able to write a good letter if they ever need to do so.
3. Display Writing Your Letter (page 92) on the overhead projector. Using the problem about the sneakers, plan a letter of complaint with the students. Take them through the three steps of organizing the letter, and use this form to outline what the final letter will say. Their final letters will be written in the format of a business letter (page 93).
4. Distribute Letter Form (page 93) to students. When the outline has been completed, inform the students they are each going to write a letter to the manufacturer—HighTime Sneaker Company, 4891 South Industry Road, Tamalpin, Illinois. Tell them to write their letters in the same format as the letter on page 93. Divide the students into cooperative learning groups and encourage them to edit each other's letters as they write them. When the letters have been written and edited, transfer them onto the computer or typewriter in the form of a business letter.
5. Discuss student success and any problems they had.

Background/Follow-Up

This activity can be repeated as many times as needed until the students understand it thoroughly. There may be students in the class who have bought a product which was faulty, and they will be happy to learn a technique for addressing their grievances about that product. Reinforce the idea that a matter-of-fact, courteous method is usually the best way to solve a problem of this sort.

Planning Your Letter

You must have a clear purpose when writing a letter of complaint. You have spent good money on a product—HighTime Sneakers—which did not perform as they should be expected to perform. The sneakers were expensive. You worked at a part-time job for weeks to pay for them. Your purpose in writing a letter of complaint will be to obtain some sort of compensation for what has been a bad deal for you because the sneakers were not as the manufacturer had advertised them to be.

You first wanted HighTime Sneakers when you saw them on television on the feet of one of your favorite sports stars. You wanted to have the same kind he had. You believed that if he was willing to go on television and tell people he wore those sneakers, it meant they were good because he wore only the best. Or so you thought.

You had looked forward to the day when you earned enough money to buy them, and you worked hard for them. After you bought them, you wore them for only one month before the soles cracked and split. You could not wear them anymore because they let the water in so your feet got wet when it rained. This was not what you expected. You expected these sneakers to be really good ones, ones that you would be able to wear for several months because that's what the manufacturer had led you to believe.

You feel the manufacturer should be expected to stand behind its product. What can you write the manufacturer which will convince him to stand by the product and either refund your money or send you a new pair of sneakers free? Here are some Do's and Don'ts to keep in mind when you write your letter.

DO . . .

- Decide exactly what you want to ask the manufacturer to do.
- List your reasons for believing you got a bad deal on the sneakers.
- Clearly tell the manufacturer why you feel you should be recompensed for sneakers on which you wasted hard-earned money.

DON'T . . .

- Get nasty.
- Make threats.
- Use bad language.

There is an old saying that you can catch more flies with honey than you can with vinegar, and you will get satisfaction by writing a letter which states your position clearly and firmly but without rancor. You want the manufacturer's representative to read your letter with concern and interest. After all, he wants your business again.

Writing Your Letter

The best letter of complaint will have about three paragraphs and will fit on one page. Outline your letter on this page, and when you have it organized exactly the way you want it to be, write it in the form of a business letter (see page 93).

Paragraph 1

- State your problem.
- List three or more facts concerning the problem.
- Show how the facts support your opinion about the problem.

Paragraph 2

- Tell what you want the manufacturer to do about the problem.
- Explain the possible consequences of your being satisfied by the manufacturer.
- State what might happen if the manufacturer does not satisfy your concerns.

Paragraph 3

Write a brief summary that restates the problem and the changes that will result from satisfying your concerns.

Letter Form

Below is a letter to the editor using the standard form for writing a business letter.

- This is the form you would use when writing a letter to the editor of a magazine.
- In the middle at the top of the page, put your name, address, and telephone number.
- On the left side of the first page, put the date, name, title, and address of the editor to whom you are writing.
- Three lines below the name and address of the person to whom you are writing, begin your letter with Dear Mr.______________, Dear Mrs.______________, or Dear Ms.______________.
- Keep your writing clear and easy to read. Remember—write for your reader!
- Sign your name at the end of the letter, under the closing word *Sincerely,* followed by a comma.

Betty Jane Smith
8888 Jenny Drive
San Jose, California 95523
(415)222-3333

January 4, 1997

Mr. Darrell E. Whitcomb, Editor
Young Times Magazine
4422 Williams Way
Carrolltown, Virginia 22110

Dear Mr. Whitcomb:

I have noticed that people are using words incorrectly, and I would like to see you do something about it.

One of the things they do is use the word "myself" when they should be using "I" instead. Yesterday I heard a man on television saying, "Myself and a friend went to the football game together." I asked my mother if this was right, and she said he should have said, "A friend and I went to the football game."

I think it's wrong for people who are on television to speak English incorrectly. Young children just learning how to talk might learn to speak incorrectly from hearing it that way on television. Do you think you could have an article in the magazine telling us how to speak correctly?

Sincerely,

Betty Jane Smith

Betty Jane Smith

Plot Plan

Three basic elements of a fiction story are *setting, character,* and *plot. Setting* refers to where and when the story takes place. *Character* refers to the people or animals in the story. And *plot* is what happens in a story. Sometimes it helps to have a picture or diagram in mind when thinking of a concept such as plot. Look at the diagram below. A story begins in a neutral place where the main character and the setting are introduced. The main character wants something or has a problem to solve. The story continues as the character meets one obstacle after another in a series of events leading to the solution of the problem. The intensity of the story grows with each event until at last the event which is most intense occurs, either through the character's own doing or the doing of someone else. The problem is solved with what is called the *climax.* The character then goes on to deal with what has happened and gets on with his life.

Plot Development

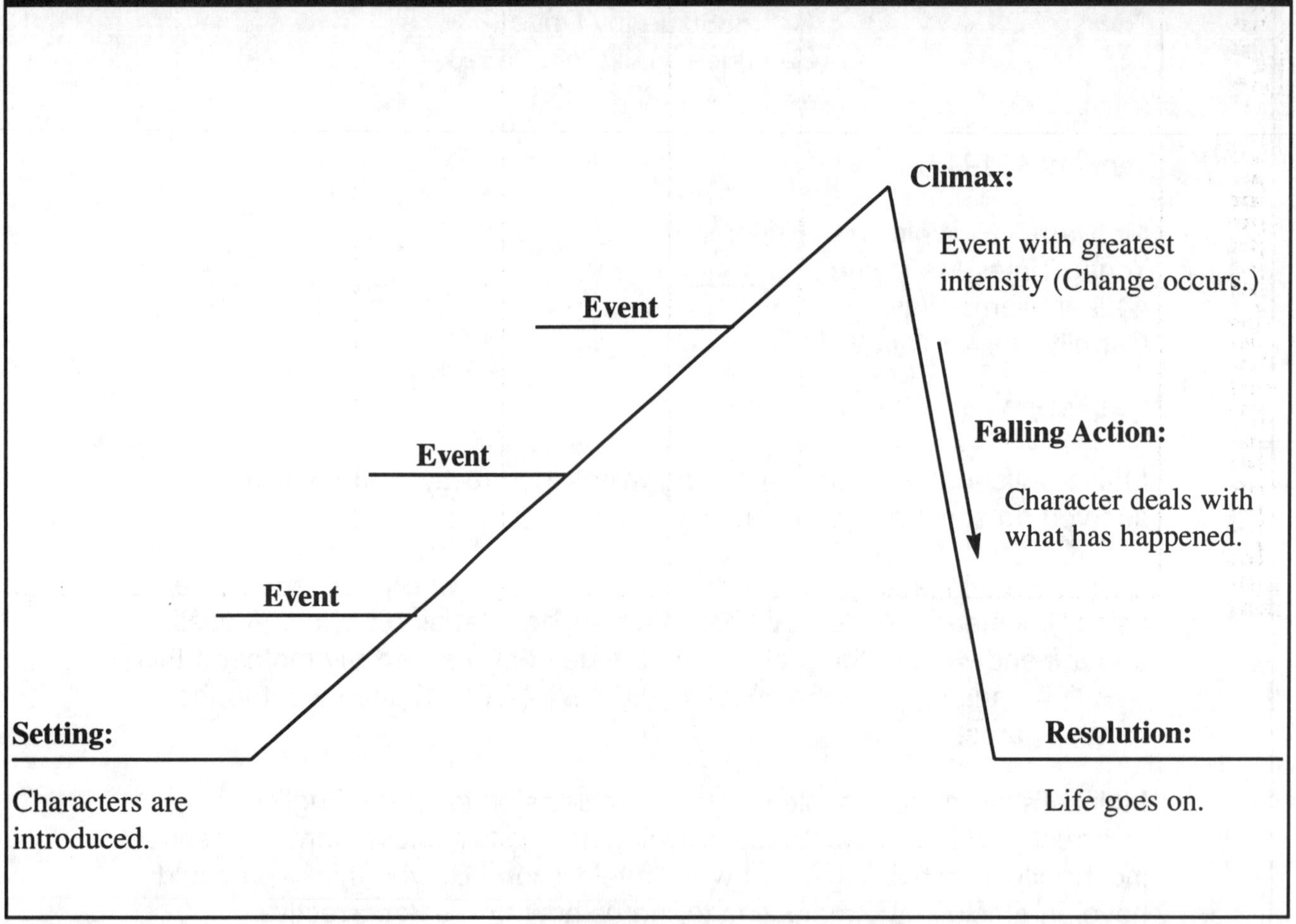

Think of it this way: The character wants to solve a problem. Something happens which causes something else, and that in turn causes something else, and so on and on. At last, something is done to solve the problem. The story winds to an end.

Brainstorming Web

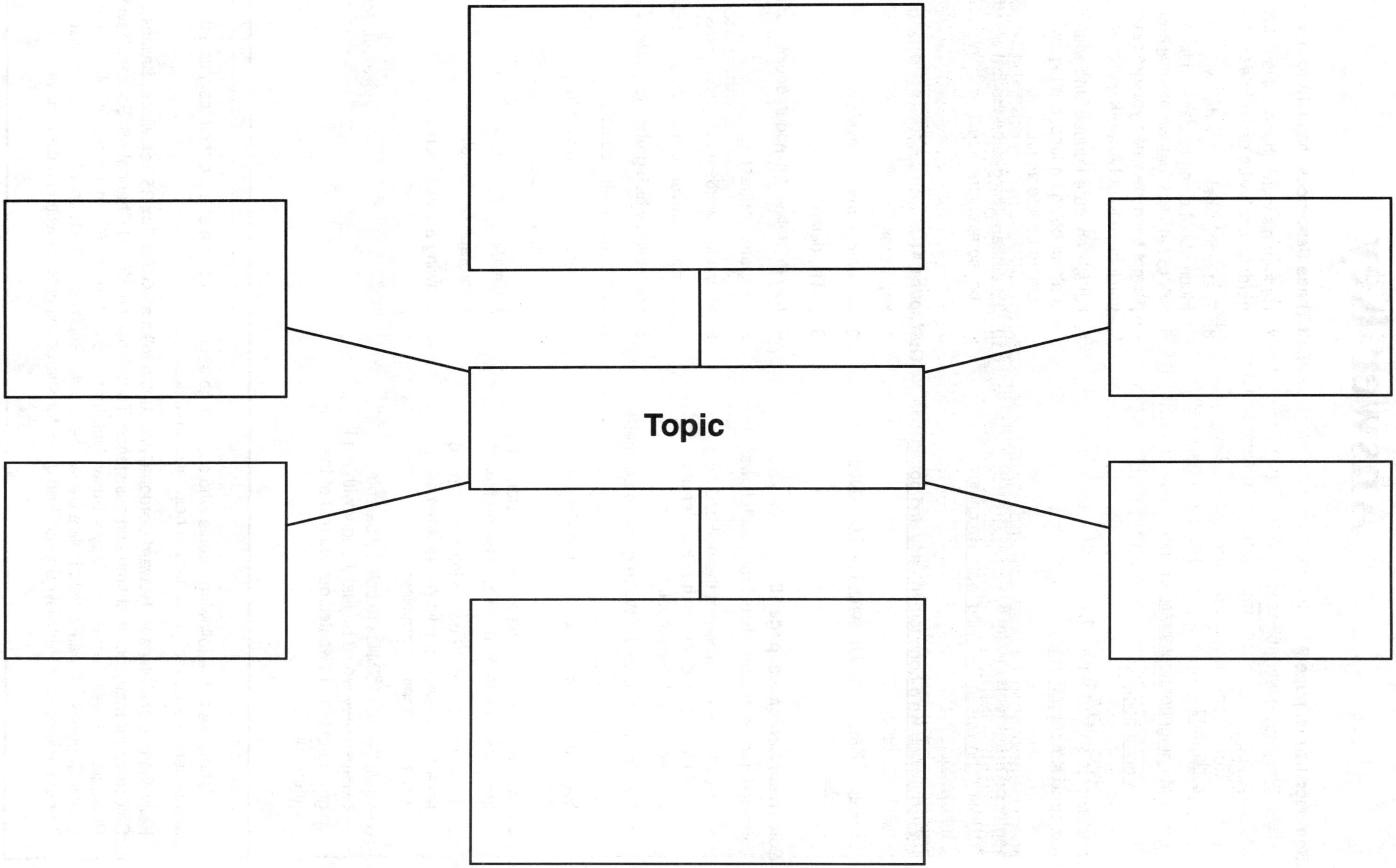

Answer Key

Sentence Cores, page 7

The people were blessed

My dad took

Bells rang

My neighbors celebrate

A good book is

Happy days are

The wind howled

Sentence Fragments, page 8

While John was in the living room watching television.

Even though we'd gone to bed early and gotten plenty of sleep.

Because Kay did well at school and got good grades.

Edit These Sentences, page 10

Corrected, the sentences should read as follows:

1. I didn't hear or notice that the bell had rung until Mary tapped me on the shoulder and pointed toward the school.
2. "Come on!" she said. "We're going to be late!"
3. We ran straight to class, and there was Mr. Miles, the principal, standing in front of the door.
4. "Why are you late?" he asked us. "Don't you know it's important to get to class on time?"
5. "I'm sorry," I said. "I got so interested in the book I was reading, I didn't hear the bell. I won't do it again! I promise!"
6. I didn't want Mr. Miles to call my parents because they would be really angry with me if I got in trouble. I sweated out the rest of the afternoon.

Edit These Sentences, page 10 *(cont.)*

7. He kept his word, though. He didn't call my parents, and I was never late for class again.
8. That night, I asked my dad why they worry so much about being to class on time. He said, "It's to help kids get into the habit of being prompt because when you get out of school, you'll have to get to work on time."
9. I'm still not sure I understand what the big deal is about being on time, but I know that I don't want to be late again.
10. It's embarrassing to be the last one through the door so everyone sees.

Quiz, page 41

1. key words
2. evaluate, examine, explain
3. justify, defend
4. narrate, relate, tell about, depict, portray
5. compare, contrast
6. to use key words as clues for ideas
7. writing whatever comes into your mind
8. something which grabs the reader's interest
9. Paragraph 1—Introduction

   Paragraph 2—Develops topic A

   Paragraph 3—Develops topic B

   Paragraph 4—Develops topic C

   Paragraph 5—Conclusion
10. Drawing a conclusion

Special thanks to the following people who spent large segments of time sharing their insights, information, and experience as real-life writers to help facilitate this book:

Kelly Nigro, Chris Manson, Howard Cordoba, and all the folks at KCBA Fox 35 Television, Salinas, California, for many hours of time and assistance; Todd Pinsky of KCCN Channel 46, Salinas; Kevin Purseglove, Press Secretary to Mayor Susan Hammer of San Jose; E. Glenn Tickner, of Microsome Inc.; Casey Coppock, of the Fairfield Police Department; Julie Robbins, EMT-1; John Gilstrap, novelist; Kathy Tolman, Principal of Parkview School, San Jose, for shared insights on writing a class novel